DBT SKILLS WORKBOOK

for

NEURODIVERGENT TEENS

Dialectical Behavioral Therapy Skills For Autistic and ADHD Teens To Master Mindfulness, Distress Tolerance, Emotional Regulation and More

SOUL SERGEANTS & DENISE SKYLER

Soul Sergeants

DISCLAIMER:

This workbook is intended as a self-help resource and should not replace professional medical advice, diagnosis, or treatment. The skills and techniques presented are based on Dialectical Behavior Therapy (DBT) principles adapted for neurodivergent teens. Individual experiences may vary. Consult a qualified mental health professional before starting any new treatment regimen. The author and publisher are not responsible for any adverse effects or consequences resulting from the use of this book.

TABLE OF CONTENT

INTRODUCTION

Jaden, a 15-year-old with ADHD, sits in class, his leg bouncing uncontrollably. The teacher's voice fades into a distant hum as his thoughts race. Suddenly, a classmate whispers, "Can you stop shaking the desk?" Jaden freezes, embarrassment and frustration flooding his system. He wants to explain, to make them understand, but the words get stuck. Instead, he spends the rest of the class fighting the urge to bolt from the room, his emotions a tangled mess he can't unravel.

Sound familiar? If you're a neurodivergent teen - whether you're autistic, have ADHD, or your brain works differently in other awesome ways - you've probably had moments like Jaden's. Moments where it feels like the world isn't built for the way your mind works.

That's exactly why this book exists. While there are plenty of DBT (Dialectical Behavior Therapy) skills books for teens out there, they often overlook the unique experiences of neurodivergent brains. This book is different. It's specially designed for teens with extraordinary minds like yours.

DBT is like a Swiss Army knife for your emotions and social interactions. It provides a set of practical skills to help you navigate the often overwhelming world of feelings, relationships, and daily challenges. These skills can be particularly helpful for neurodivergent brains, which often experience emotions and social situations more intensely.

I wrote this book because DBT changed my life, and I believe it can change yours too. Whether you're autistic or an ADHDer like me, or you just feel like your emotions are constantly getting the better of you, this book is for you. It's for anyone who's ever felt overwhelmed by their feelings, anyone who's struggled to maintain relationships, anyone who's looked in the mirror and thought, "There's gotta be a better way to live than this."

Well, there is. And you're holding it in your hands right now.

In this book, we'll explore four key areas:

1. Mindfulness: Techniques to anchor yourself in the present moment when your thoughts are racing or you're feeling overwhelmed.
2. Distress Tolerance: Strategies to handle tough situations without making them worse - perfect for those times when everything feels like too much.
3. Emotion Regulation: Tools to understand and manage your feelings, especially useful when emotions feel extra intense.
4. Interpersonal Effectiveness: Skills to navigate relationships and communication, which can sometimes be tricky with a neurodivergent brain.

Each section is packed with exercises and strategies tailored specifically for neurodivergent teens. We'll use real-life examples you can relate to, explained in a way that makes sense for your unique way of thinking.

This book isn't just for teens, though. If you're a parent, teacher, or guardian of a neurodivergent teen, you'll find valuable insights here too. Understanding these skills can help you better support the remarkable neurodivergent teens in your life.

Remember, your neurodivergent brain is a superpower, not a weakness. Yes, it comes with challenges, but it also gives you unique strengths and perspectives. This book is all about helping you harness those strengths while giving you tools to navigate the tough stuff.

I've tried to make this workbook as practical and down-to-earth as possible. You won't find a bunch of psychobabble or highfalutin' language here. Just straight talk, real strategies, and a healthy dose of "been there, done that" empathy.

Are you ready to dive in? Let's discover how DBT skills can help you thrive as a neurodivergent teen in a neurotypical world. These skills have the power to transform lives - and they can make a big difference for you too.
Let's get started.

How to Use This Workbook

First things first: this isn't a race. You're not going to read this book cover to cover in one sitting and emerge a DBT master. (And if you do, please tell me your secrets because I'd love to learn about that superpower.)

Instead, think of this workbook as a journey. A really important journey that's going to take time, effort, and yeah, probably some tears along the way. But trust me, it's worth it.

Here's how I suggest approaching this workbook:

1. Start at the beginning: I know, groundbreaking advice, right? But seriously, the skills in this book build on each other. Don't skip ahead, no matter how tempting it might be.

2. Do the exercises: I can't stress this enough. Reading about DBT skills is great, but actually doing them is where the magic happens. It's like learning to ride a bike - you can read about pedaling all day long, but at some point, you gotta get on the damn bike.

3. Be patient with yourself: You're going to mess up. You're going to have days where it feels like you're not making any progress. That's okay. It's normal. Be kind to yourself on those days.

4. Practice, practice, practice: DBT skills are just that - skills. And like any skill, they get better with practice. So keep at it, even when it feels tough.

5. Personalize it: This workbook is a guide, not a rulebook. If a certain exercise doesn't resonate with you, that's cool. Tweak it. Make it your own. The goal is to find what works for you.

6. Get support: If you're working with a therapist, awesome. Share this workbook with them. If not, consider finding a DBT skills group or an online community. This journey is tough, but you don't have to do it alone.

DBT and Neurodivergence: A Powerful Combination

When I first started learning about DBT, I felt like I was trying to fit a square peg into a round hole. See, I'm neurodivergent. My brain doesn't always work the way society expects it to. And for a long time, I thought that meant DBT wasn't for me.

Boy, was I wrong.

Here's the thing: DBT isn't about changing who you are. It's about giving you tools to navigate a world that isn't always built for brains like ours. And let me tell you, these tools can be especially powerful for neurodivergent folks.

Take mindfulness, for example. If you're on the autism spectrum or have ADHD, you might find that your mind races a million miles a minute. Mindfulness can help you slow down, focus, and find a moment of calm in the chaos.

Or consider emotional regulation. If you're neurodivergent, you might experience emotions more intensely than neurotypical folks. DBT doesn't try to squash those emotions - instead, it gives you strategies to ride them out without getting overwhelmed.

Throughout this workbook, I've included specific tips and adaptations for neurodivergent individuals. Because I believe that DBT can be a game-changer for us, but sometimes we need to adjust the game a little bit.

So if you're neurodivergent, know this: you belong here. This journey is for you too. Your unique brain isn't an obstacle - it's an asset. And with the right tools, you can harness its power in amazing ways.

A Personal Note

Before we dive into the meat of this workbook, I want to share something with you. A few years ago, I was in a really dark place. My emotions felt like they were controlling me, not the other way around. My relationships were a mess. I was impulsive, angry, and scared.

One night, things got really bad. I won't go into the details, but let's just say I hit rock bottom. And as I sat there, feeling more alone than I ever had in my life, I made a decision. I decided that I wasn't going to let my emotions run the show anymore. I was going to fight back.

That's when I really committed to DBT. And slowly but surely, things started to change. It wasn't easy. There were days when I wanted to give up. Days when I backslid into old habits. But I kept at it. And you know what? It worked. Today, I'm not perfect (spoiler alert: nobody is), but I'm so much better equipped to handle life's challenges. I have healthier relationships. I can regulate my emotions. I can sit with discomfort without feeling like I'm going to explode.

I'm telling you this because I want you to know that change is possible. No matter how hopeless things might feel right now, there is a path forward. And this workbook? It's your map for that journey.

So, are you ready to get started? To learn some kick-ass skills that'll help you navigate life's stormy seas? To discover strength inside yourself that you never knew you had? Yeah? Let's do this thing.

-Denise Skyler

CHAPTER 1
Understanding DBT for Neurodivergent Teens

Chapter 1.1

What is DBT?

You're probably wondering, "What the heck is DBT?" Don't worry, we're going to break it down together. By the end of this chapter, you'll have a solid grasp on what DBT is all about and why it might just be your new secret weapon for navigating life.

So, what is DBT?

DBT stands for Dialectical Behavior Therapy. I know, I know – that's a mouthful. Let's break it down:

Dialectical: This fancy word basically means "two opposite ideas can be true at the same time." We'll dive deeper into this soon, but for now, think of it like this: You can be doing your best AND still have room to improve. Both can be true at once.

Behavior: This part's pretty straightforward. DBT focuses on changing behaviors – the things we do and how we react to stuff.

Therapy: A way of helping people deal with mental or emotional problems.

Put it all together, and DBT is a type of therapy that helps people change their behaviors while accepting that opposite ideas can both be true. It's like learning to juggle – you're keeping multiple things in the air at once, but with practice, it gets easier.

A Brief History Lesson (Don't Worry, It's Short!)

DBT was created by a psychologist named Marsha Linehan in the late

1980s. Marsha developed DBT because she found that regular talk therapy wasn't helping people with really intense emotions and self-destructive behaviors. She wanted to find a way to help people accept themselves as they are while also working on changing the behaviors that were causing them problems.

Here's a cool fact: Marsha later revealed that she herself struggled with intense emotions and self-harm. She created DBT not just as a therapist, but as someone who really understood what it's like to feel overwhelmed by your own mind. Pretty awesome, right?

Why DBT for Neurodivergent Teens?

Now, you might be thinking, "Okay, but what does this have to do with me being autistic or having ADHD?" Great question! While DBT wasn't originally created specifically for neurodivergent folks, it turns out that a lot of the skills it teaches are super helpful for people with autism and ADHD.

Think about it:

1. If you're autistic, you might sometimes struggle with understanding social cues or managing sensory overload. DBT can help you develop strategies to navigate social situations and cope with overwhelming sensory experiences.

2. If you have ADHD, you might find it hard to focus, control impulses, or manage your emotions. DBT offers techniques to improve focus, think before acting, and regulate your feelings.

3. For both autism and ADHD, DBT can help with things like:
   - Dealing with anxiety and depression (which often go hand-in-hand with neurodivergence)
   - Improving communication with others
   - Building self-esteem and self-acceptance
   - Managing meltdowns or shutdowns
   - Developing healthy coping mechanisms

The Four Pillars of DBT

DBT is built on four main skill areas. Think of them like the four legs of a table – they all work together to keep you stable and supported. Here's a quick overview:

1. Mindfulness: Being aware of the present moment without judgment. It's like developing a superpower that lets you tune into what's happening right now, both inside and outside of you.

2. Distress Tolerance: Learning to handle tough situations without making them worse. It's like having a mental emergency kit for when life gets really hard.

3. Emotion Regulation: Understanding and managing your emotions. Think of it as becoming the boss of your feelings instead of letting them boss you around.

4. Interpersonal Effectiveness: Improving your relationships and communication skills. It's about learning to express your needs, set boundaries, and connect with others in healthy ways.

We'll dive deep into each of these skills throughout this workbook, but for now, just know that they're the building blocks of DBT.

The DBT Mindset: Acceptance and Change

Remember when we talked about "dialectical" earlier? This is where it really comes into play. DBT is all about balancing two seemingly opposite ideas: accepting yourself as you are AND working to change.

Let's break this down with an example:

Imagine you're having trouble making friends at school. The acceptance part of DBT would encourage you to acknowledge that social situations are genuinely challenging for you, and that's okay. You're not "broken" or "wrong" for finding this difficult.

At the same time, the change part of DBT would help you learn and practice social skills to make connecting with others easier. You're accepting your current struggle while also working to improve.

It's like saying, "I accept that this is hard for me right now, AND I'm going to learn ways to make it easier." Both parts are equally important.

This balance is crucial for neurodivergent teens. It's about embracing your unique brain while also developing skills to thrive in a world that's not always built for minds like ours.

How DBT Looks in Practice

So, what does actually doing DBT look like? Great question! DBT typically involves a few different components:

1. Individual Therapy: One-on-one sessions with a therapist where you work on your specific challenges and goals.

2. Group Skills Training: Classes where you learn and practice DBT skills with other people. It's like a fun (yes, really!) skill-building workshop.

3. Phone Coaching: Some DBT programs offer phone support to help you use your skills in real-life situations.

4. Homework: Don't groan! This isn't like school homework. It's more like practicing a new video game move until you've got it down.

In this workbook, we'll be focusing mainly on the skills training part. You'll learn tons of practical techniques and have plenty of chances to practice them.

Why DBT Works: The Science Behind It

I promise I won't get too nerdy here, but it's pretty cool to know that there's solid science backing up DBT. Research has shown that DBT can help with a whole bunch of things, including:

- Reducing anxiety and depression
- Improving emotion regulation
- Decreasing self-harm behaviors
- Enhancing relationships and social skills
- Boosting self-esteem and self-compassion

For neurodivergent teens specifically, studies have found that DBT can help with:

- Reducing meltdowns and shutdowns
- Improving focus and attention
- Enhancing communication skills
- Developing better coping strategies for sensory issues
- Increasing overall quality of life

The best part? Your brain is super adaptable (scientists call this "neuroplasticity"). By practicing DBT skills, you're literally rewiring your brain to be more resilient and emotionally balanced. How cool is that?

DBT in Real Life: A Day in the Life

To give you a better idea of how DBT might fit into your life, let's walk through a typical day with DBT skills:

Morning: You wake up feeling anxious about a big test. Instead of letting your worries spiral, you use a mindfulness technique to ground yourself in the present moment. You notice your anxious thoughts without getting caught up in them.

At School: During lunch, you feel overwhelmed by the noisy cafeteria. You use a distress tolerance skill called "TIPP" (we'll learn about this later!) to help calm your nervous system. You're able to stay and eat with your friends instead of having to leave.

Bedtime: As you're trying to sleep, your mind starts racing with thoughts about all the things you need to do tomorrow. You use a mindfulness technique to gently bring your attention back to your breath, helping you relax and fall asleep.

See how these skills can weave into your everyday life? With practice, they become second nature – like having a trusty toolbox you can reach into whenever you need it.

Your DBT Journey Starts Here

Alright, future DBT master, you've made it through the crash course on what DBT is all about. Give yourself a high five (or a quiet mental nod if you're not into high fives) – you've taken the first step on an awesome journey.

As we dive into the specific skills in the coming chapters, remember:

1. This is your journey. Take it at your own pace.
2. It's okay if some skills feel weird or hard at first. That's normal!
3. Be kind to yourself. You're learning and growing, and that's amazing.
4. Your neurodivergent brain is a superpower. DBT is here to help you harness it.

Before we wrap up, let's do a quick check-in. Take a moment to reflect on these questions:

What's one thing you learned about DBT that surprised you?

Can you think of a situation in your life where DBT skills might be helpful?

What are you most excited about learning as we continue?

Awesome job! You're officially starting your DBT journey. In the next chapter, we'll dive into our first skill area: Mindfulness. Get ready to develop some serious mental superpowers!

Remember, you've got this. Your brain is unique and amazing, and with DBT in your toolkit, you're about to become even more awesome. Let's do this!

Chapter 1.2:

DBT and Neurodivergence: Tailoring the Approach

In this section, we're going to explore how DBT can be tailored to fit your neurodivergent mind, making it a powerful tool in your life-skills toolkit.

Understanding Neurodivergence

Before we jump into the nitty-gritty of DBT and neurodivergence, let's take a moment to celebrate what it means to be neurodivergent. Being neurodivergent means your brain processes information differently from what society considers "typical." It's like having a computer that runs on a unique operating system – not better or worse, just different.

For you, this might mean:

1. You're autistic: Your brain might be extra good at noticing details, diving deep into your interests, or thinking outside the box. You might also find some social situations or sensory experiences challenging.

2. You have ADHD: Your brain might be super creative, great at thinking on your feet, or excellent at hyperfocusing on things you love. You might also struggle with staying organized or sitting still for long periods.

3. You're both autistic and have ADHD: You've got a double scoop of neurodiversity, which comes with its own unique blend of strengths and challenges.

Remember, neurodivergence isn't a flaw or something to be "fixed." It's a natural variation in human brains, and it comes with its own set of superpowers. DBT isn't here to change who you are – it's here to help you navigate the world more easily while embracing your awesome neurodivergent self.

The Neurodivergent Experience and DBT

Now, let's talk about how being neurodivergent might impact your experience with DBT. Here are some common experiences that many neurodivergent teens have, and how DBT can help:

1. Sensory Sensitivities:
Many autistic teens (and some with ADHD) experience sensory input more intensely. Sounds might seem louder, lights brighter, or textures more noticeable.

How DBT can help: Mindfulness skills can teach you to observe these sensations without getting overwhelmed by them. Distress tolerance skills can provide strategies for coping when sensory input becomes too much.

2. Executive Function Challenges:
Both autism and ADHD can make things like organization, time management, and task initiation tricky.

How DBT can help: The structure and routine of DBT can improve executive function. Skills like breaking tasks into smaller steps and using mindfulness to improve focus can be game-changers.

3. Emotional Intensity:
Many neurodivergent teens experience emotions very deeply and may have trouble regulating them.

How DBT can help: Emotion regulation skills are a core part of DBT. You'll learn to identify, understand, and manage your emotions more effectively.

4. Social Communication Differences:
Autistic teens often have a different way of communicating and understanding social cues. ADHD can sometimes lead to impulsive social behaviors.

How DBT can help: Interpersonal effectiveness skills can provide clear, concrete strategies for navigating social situations and improving communication.

5. Difficulty with Change:
Many neurodivergent individuals prefer routine and may struggle with unexpected changes.

How DBT can help: Distress tolerance skills can provide strategies for coping with change and uncertainty. Mindfulness can help you stay grounded when things feel unpredictable.

6. Hyperfocus and Special Interests:
Both autism and ADHD can involve intense focus on particular topics or activities.

How DBT can help: While this trait can be a strength, DBT can help you learn to shift your attention when needed and find balance in your activities.

Real-Life Example: DBT in Action for a Neurodivergent Teen

Let's look at how this might play out in real life. Meet Alex:

Alex is a 15-year-old autistic teen who also has ADHD. He loves video games and has an encyclopedic knowledge of marine biology. Alex often feels overwhelmed at school, especially during lunch when the cafeteria is noisy and crowded. He sometimes has meltdowns at home when plans change unexpectedly.

Here's how Alex might use DBT skills, tailored to his neurodivergent brain:

1. Mindfulness:
Alex learns to use his special interest in marine biology as a mindfulness anchor. When feeling overwhelmed, he visualizes being underwater, focusing on imaginary fish swimming by. This helps him stay present and calm without relying on uncomfortable bodily sensations.

2. Distress Tolerance:
To cope with the noisy cafeteria, Alex creates a "sensory emergency kit" with noise-canceling headphones, a stress ball with an interesting texture, and a card with written steps for a calming visualization. This gives him concrete tools to use when feeling overwhelmed.

3. Emotion Regulation:
Alex struggles to identify emotions, so he creates a "feelings chart" using characters from his favorite video game. Each character represents a different emotion, making it easier for Alex to recognize and name what he's feeling.

4. Interpersonal Effectiveness:
To practice assertiveness, Alex role-plays conversations using characters from his favorite TV show. This makes the practice more engaging and helps Alex remember the skills more easily.

By tailoring DBT skills to fit his neurodivergent brain, Alex is able to reduce meltdowns, cope better with sensory challenges, and communicate more effectively with friends and family.

The Power of Self-Advocacy in DBT

As a neurodivergent teen using DBT, one of your most powerful tools will be self-advocacy. This means speaking up for your needs and helping others understand how to support you best. Here are some ways you can practice self-advocacy in your DBT journey:

1. Communicate Your Needs:
If a particular exercise or technique doesn't work for you, speak up! Let your therapist, group leader, or support person know. For example, "I find it hard to focus on my breath. Could we try a visual mindfulness exercise instead?"

2. Ask for Clarification:
If something isn't clear, it's okay to ask for more explanation or examples. You might say, "I'm not sure I understand. Could you explain that in a different way or give me a specific example?"

3. Request Accommodations:
If you need certain accommodations to participate fully in DBT, don't hesitate to ask. This might include things like:
- Taking breaks during long sessions
- Having written instructions for exercises
- Using fidget tools during sessions
- Adjusting the lighting or seating arrangement

4. Share Your Perspective:
Your unique way of seeing the world is valuable! Share your insights and experiences. You might notice connections or applications of DBT skills that others haven't thought of.

5. Educate Others:
Many people might not understand what it means to be neurodivergent. When you feel comfortable, sharing your experiences can help others learn and be more supportive.

Remember, self-advocacy is a skill that gets stronger with practice. It's okay if it feels awkward or scary at first. Each time you speak up for yourself, you're not only improving your own experience but also paving the way for other neurodivergent individuals.

Embracing Your Neurodivergent Strengths in DBT

While we've talked a lot about challenges, it's crucial to remember that being neurodivergent comes with many strengths that can be super helpful in your DBT journey. Let's explore some of these:

1. Attention to Detail:
Many neurodivergent individuals have an amazing ability to notice small details. This can be super helpful in mindfulness practices and in observing your thoughts and emotions.

2. Pattern Recognition:
If you're good at spotting patterns, you might excel at recognizing triggers for certain emotions or behaviors. This can be a huge asset in emotion regulation and distress tolerance work.

3. Hyperfocus:
While it can sometimes be challenging, the ability to focus intensely on something can be a superpower when learning new DBT skills. Once you're interested in a skill, you might become an expert at it!

4. Out-of-the-Box Thinking:
Many neurodivergent folks are great at coming up with unique solutions to problems. This creativity can help you adapt DBT skills to fit your needs and even come up with new ways to use them.

5. Passion and Enthusiasm:
When neurodivergent individuals get interested in something, they often pursue it with incredible passion. If you can connect with DBT, your enthusiasm could drive you to make amazing progress.

6. Honesty and Directness:
Many autistic individuals value honesty and direct communication. This can be a real strength in DBT, where being honest about your experiences and needs is super important.

7. Resilience:
Navigating a world that's not always designed for your brain has likely made you pretty resilient. This resilience can help you persist with DBT even when it's challenging.

Wrapping Up: Your Neurodivergent DBT Journey

We've covered a lot in this chapter! Let's do a quick recap:

1. Being neurodivergent means your brain works in unique and valuable ways.
2. DBT can be super helpful for neurodivergent teens, but it might need some tweaks to work best for you.
3. We'll use strategies like visual aids, concrete examples, and special interest integration to make DBT more accessible.
4. Self-advocacy is a powerful tool in your DBT journey.
5. Your neurodivergent traits bring many strengths to the table in DBT.

Remember, this workbook is a tool for you to use in a way that works best for your unique brain. There's no one "right" way to do DBT. As we go through the skills in the coming chapters, feel free to adapt, modify, and personalize them to fit your needs.

Before we move on, take a moment to reflect on these questions:

What are three strengths you have that might help you in learning DBT skills?

Can you think of a situation where you might need to self-advocate in your DBT journey?

Chapter 1.3:

The Four Core Skills Modules

In this section, we're going to explore the four core skills modules that make up the backbone of DBT. Think of these modules as your superhero training program – each one giving you a different power to tackle life's challenges.

Now, I know what you might be thinking: "Four modules? That sounds like a lot!" Don't worry, we're going to break it down step by step. By the end of this section, you'll have a solid grasp of what each module is about and how it can help your neurodivergent brain thrive.

So, what are these four magical modules? Drum roll, please...

1. Mindfulness
2. Distress Tolerance
3. Emotion Regulation
4. Interpersonal Effectiveness

Let's look into each one and see how they can work for your unique brain.

1. Mindfulness: Your Superpower of Present Moment Awareness

Imagine you had a pause button for your brain. A way to step back from the chaos of thoughts and feelings and just... be. That's what mindfulness is all about.

For neurodivergent teens, mindfulness can be a game-changer. Here's why:

- If you have ADHD, your mind might feel like it's constantly racing from one thought to another. Mindfulness can help you slow down and focus on one thing at a time.
- If you're autistic, you might sometimes feel overwhelmed by sensory input or social situations. Mindfulness can help you ground yourself and manage those overwhelming feelings.

But here's the cool part – mindfulness isn't about forcing your mind to be quiet. It's about observing your thoughts and feelings without getting caught up in them. It's like watching clouds pass by in the sky – you see them, but you don't have to chase after them.

Real-life example: Meet Jamie. Jamie is a 16-year-old with ADHD who often feels overwhelmed at school. When things get tough, Jamie uses a quick mindfulness technique:

1. Jamie takes a deep breath and focuses on the sensation of air entering and leaving their lungs.
2. They notice five things they can see around them.
3. They identify four things they can touch.
4. They listen for three distinct sounds.
5. They try to smell two different scents.
6. Finally, they notice one thing they can taste.

This "5-4-3-2-1" technique helps Jamie ground themselves in the present moment, reducing anxiety and improving focus.

2. Distress Tolerance: Your Shield Against Life's Storms

Life can throw some pretty intense curveballs our way. Distress tolerance skills are like your personal shield and sword to face these challenges head-on.

For neurodivergent teens, distress tolerance can be particularly helpful:

- If you're autistic, unexpected changes or sensory overload can be really distressing. These skills can help you cope when things don't go

as planned.
- If you have ADHD, you might sometimes act impulsively when you're upset. Distress tolerance skills can give you strategies to pause and respond more effectively.

Distress tolerance isn't about making bad situations good. It's about learning to survive and even grow from difficult experiences without making things worse.

3. Emotion Regulation: Becoming the Boss of Your Feelings

Emotions can sometimes feel like wild horses – powerful and hard to control. Emotion regulation skills teach you how to become an expert horse trainer, guiding your emotions instead of being dragged along by them.

For neurodivergent teens, emotion regulation can be a superpower:

- If you're autistic, you might sometimes feel emotions very intensely or have trouble identifying what you're feeling. These skills can help you understand and manage your emotions more effectively.
- If you have ADHD, your emotions might feel like they change quickly or are hard to control. Emotion regulation can give you tools to ride the waves of your feelings without wiping out.

Emotion regulation isn't about suppressing your feelings. It's about understanding them, expressing them in healthy ways, and not letting them control your actions.

Let's look at another example: Meet Zoe. Zoe is a 15-year-old with ADHD who often feels intense anger that leads to arguments with family and friends. Here's how Zoe uses emotion regulation skills:

1. Zoe notices she's starting to feel angry (her heart is racing and her fists are clenched).
2. She pauses and asks herself, "What triggered this feeling?"
3. Zoe realizes she's angry because she feels her opinion wasn't heard in a group project.

4. Instead of lashing out, she takes a few deep breaths and counts to ten.
5. Zoe then uses "I feel" statements to express herself calmly: "I feel frustrated because I don't think my ideas are being considered."

By using these emotion regulation techniques, Zoe is able to express her feelings without damaging her relationships.

4. Interpersonal Effectiveness: Your Guide to Navigating the Social World

Relationships can be tricky for everyone, but they can be especially challenging for neurodivergent teens. Interpersonal effectiveness skills are like your personal GPS for the social world, helping you navigate relationships more smoothly.

Here's why these skills are so valuable for neurodivergent teens:

- If you're autistic, you might sometimes struggle to read social cues or know how to respond in social situations. These skills give you concrete strategies for communication and relationship-building.
- If you have ADHD, you might sometimes speak impulsively or have trouble maintaining focus in conversations. Interpersonal effectiveness skills can help you communicate more clearly and effectively.

Interpersonal effectiveness isn't about changing who you are or masking your neurodivergent traits. It's about learning to express your needs, set boundaries, and connect with others in ways that work for you.

Putting It All Together: Your DBT Toolkit

Now that we've explored each module, you might be wondering how they all fit together. Think of these four skills as different tools in your mental health toolkit. Just like you wouldn't use a hammer for every job around the house, you won't use the same DBT skill for every situation in life.

- You might use mindfulness to notice when you're getting upset (emotion regulation).
- Then you could use distress tolerance skills to calm down in the moment.
- Finally, you might use interpersonal effectiveness skills to communicate your feelings to someone else.

As you learn and practice these skills, you'll get better at knowing which tool to use when. It's like becoming a mental health handyperson!

Adapting DBT Skills for Your Neurodivergent Brain

Remember we mentioned earlier that DBT wasn't originally created with neurodivergent brains in mind. But that doesn't mean it can't be super helpful for you! Throughout this workbook, we'll explore ways to adapt each skill to work better for autistic and ADHD brains.

For example:

- If traditional mindfulness exercises feel uncomfortable, we might explore mindful movement or using special interests as a focus point.
- For emotion regulation, we might use visual aids or special interest themes to help identify and understand feelings.
- In interpersonal effectiveness, we'll discuss how to advocate for your needs as a neurodivergent person.

The key is to be patient with yourself and willing to experiment. What works for one person might not work for another, and that's okay! This workbook is all about finding the strategies that work best for your unique brain.

Wrapping Up: Your DBT Journey Begins

Whew! We've covered a lot in this chapter. Let's do a quick recap:

1. Mindfulness: Your superpower of present moment awareness
2. Distress Tolerance: Your shield against life's storms

3. Emotion Regulation: Becoming the boss of your feelings
4. Interpersonal Effectiveness: Your guide to navigating the social world

These four modules work together to give you a comprehensive set of skills for managing emotions, relationships, and life's challenges.

Before we move on, take a moment to reflect on these questions:

Which of the four modules are you most excited to learn more about?

Can you think of a recent situation where one of these skills might have been helpful?

What's one way you might need to adapt these skills to work better for your neurodivergent brain?

Awesome job! You're already starting to think about how these skills can apply to your life. In the coming chapters, we'll dive deep into each module, exploring specific techniques and how to make them work for you.

Always remember, learning DBT skills is a journey, not a destination. Be patient with yourself, celebrate small victories, and don't be afraid to ask for help when you need it. Your neurodivergent brain is powerful and unique, and with these DBT skills in your toolkit, you're about to become even more awesome.

CHAPTER 2
Mindfulness Skills

Chapter 2.1

"What" Skills: Observing, Describing, Participating

In the first chapter, you covered a great mile from learning the basics of DBT to how DBT fits your unique brain. Now, we're about to sail together into the "What" skills of mindfulness: Observing, Describing, and Participating. These skills are like your secret weapons for tuning into the world around you and inside you. They're called "What" skills because they answer the question, "What am I doing?" when practicing mindfulness.

Now, I know what you might be thinking: "Mindfulness? Isn't that just sitting still and thinking about nothing?" Nope! It's way cooler than that, especially for our neurodivergent brains. Let's break it down.

Observing: Becoming a Detective of Your Own Experience

Imagine you're a detective, but instead of solving crimes, you're investigating your own experiences. That's what observing is all about. It's noticing what's happening around you and inside you without trying to change it.

For neurodivergent teens, observing can be super helpful:

- If you have ADHD, your mind might often feel like a busy highway. Observing helps you notice your thoughts without getting caught up in the traffic.

- If you're autistic, you might sometimes feel overwhelmed by sensory input. Observing can help you notice sensations without immediately reacting to them.

Here's how to practice observing:

1. Pick something to focus on. It could be your breath, a sound, or even a fidget toy.
2. Notice what you're experiencing through your senses. What do you see, hear, smell, taste, or feel?
3. When your mind wanders (and it will – that's totally normal!), gently bring your attention back to what you're observing.

Let's try a quick observing exercise:

Take a moment to look around the room you're in. Notice five things you can see. Don't judge them or think too much about them – just observe. Maybe you see a blue chair, a scratched desk, a poster on the wall, a plant in the corner, and a stack of books.

How was that? You just practiced observing!

Describing: Putting Your Experience into Words

Now that you've observed something, the next step is describing it. This means putting your experience into words, like you're reporting the facts without adding judgments or interpretations.

Describing can be especially useful for neurodivergent teens:

- If you're autistic, you might sometimes struggle to express what you're feeling. Describing helps you put words to your experiences.
- If you have ADHD, your thoughts might sometimes feel jumbled. Describing can help you organize your thoughts and communicate them more clearly.

Here's how to practice describing:

1. Start with what you observed.
2. Use simple, factual statements to describe it.
3. Avoid adding judgments or interpretations.

Let's try a describing exercise:

Think about how you're feeling right now. Instead of just saying "I feel bad" or "I feel good," try to describe the sensation in more detail. For example:

"My shoulders feel tense."
"My breathing is shallow and quick."
"I feel a fluttery sensation in my stomach."

See how that gives a clearer picture of what you're experiencing?

Participating: Diving Fully into the Moment

Participating is about fully engaging in whatever you're doing, without self-consciousness or second-guessing. It's like when you're so into a video game or a book that you forget everything else – that's participating!

For neurodivergent teens, participating can be a game-changer:

- If you're autistic, you might sometimes feel disconnected from what's happening around you. Participating helps you engage more fully with your environment and the people in it.
- If you have ADHD, you might struggle with staying focused on one thing. Participating can help you immerse yourself in an activity and stay present.

Here's how to practice participating:

1. Choose an activity – it could be anything from eating a meal to playing a game.
2. Engage in the activity fully, using all your senses.
3. If you notice your mind wandering, gently bring your attention back to the activity.

Let's try a participating exercise:

Next time you eat a meal, try to participate fully in the experience. Notice the colors and textures of the food. Pay attention to the taste and how it changes as you chew. Feel the sensations in your mouth and throat as you swallow. Hear any sounds you make while eating.

Making "What" Skills Work for Your Neurodivergent Brain

Now, I know these skills might sound simple, but they can be challenging, especially for neurodivergent brains. Here are some tips to make them work better for you:

1. Start Small: Don't try to observe, describe, or participate for long periods at first. Even a few seconds of mindful awareness is a win!

2. Use Your Interests: If you have a special interest, use it in your mindfulness practice. For example, if you love space, you could observe and describe the night sky.

3. Make It Sensory: Use fidget toys, textured objects, or other sensory tools to help you stay focused during mindfulness exercises.

4. Be Kind to Yourself: Your mind will wander, and that's okay. Mindfulness isn't about having a perfectly quiet mind – it's about noticing when your mind wanders and gently bringing it back.

5. Adapt for Sensory Needs: If certain sensations are uncomfortable for you, it's okay to adjust. For example, if focusing on your breath feels uncomfortable, you could focus on the sensation of your feet on the ground instead.

Challenges and Troubleshooting

Let's be real – practicing these skills isn't always easy. Here are some common challenges and how to handle them:

1. "My mind won't stop racing!"
   This is super common, especially if you have ADHD. Remember, the goal isn't to stop your thoughts – it's to notice them. Each time you notice your mind has wandered, that's mindfulness in action!

2. "I feel silly doing this."
It can feel weird at first, especially if you're not used to paying such close attention to your experiences. That's normal! Try practicing in private until you feel more comfortable.

3. "I can't sit still to do this."
Good news – you don't have to! You can practice these skills while moving. Try observing and describing what you experience during a walk, or participate fully while doing a favorite physical activity.

4. "I keep getting lost in my thoughts."
Welcome to being human! When you notice you've gotten lost in thought, just gently bring your attention back to what you're observing, describing, or participating in. Each time you do this, you're strengthening your mindfulness muscles.

5. "I don't think I'm doing it right."
There's no "right" way to do mindfulness. As long as you're attempting to observe, describe, or participate, you're practicing the skills. It gets easier with time, I promise!

Wrapping Up: Your "What" Skills Toolkit

Awesome job making it through this chapter! Let's do a quick recap:

1. Observing: Noticing your experiences without trying to change them.
2. Describing: Putting your observations into words without judgement.
3. Participating: Fully engaging in the present moment.

These "What" skills are your foundation for mindfulness. They help you tune into your experiences, communicate more clearly, and engage more fully with life.

Mindfulness is a practice. It's not about being perfect – it's about showing up and trying. Each time you use these skills, even for a few seconds, you're building your mindfulness muscles.

Before we wrap up, let's do a quick reflection. Take a moment to answer these questions:

Which of the "What" skills do you think will be most helpful for you?

Can you think of a situation in your daily life where you could practice one of these skills?

What's one way you might need to adapt these skills to work better for your neurodivergent brain?

Exercise 1: Sensory Scavenger Hunt

Let's practice your observing skills with a fun sensory scavenger hunt!

Instructions:
1. Set a timer for 5 minutes.

2. In the space below, list:

5 things you can see

4 things you can touch

3 things you can hear

Exercise 1: Sensory Scavenger Hunt

2 things you can smell

1 thing you can taste (if safe and appropriate)

Exercise 2: Emotion Weather Report

Let's practice describing your emotional state like a weather report.

Instructions:
1. Take a moment to check in with yourself.
2. In the space below, describe your current emotional state as if you were a weather reporter. For example, "Today's emotional forecast shows scattered anxiety clouds with a chance of excitement in the afternoon."

My Emotion Weather Report:

Chapter 2.2

"How" Skills: Non-judgmentally, One-mindfully, Effectively

Think of it this way: if the "What" skills are about what you're doing (observing, describing, participating), the "How" skills are about how you're doing it. Let's break it down and see how these skills can work for your unique neurodivergent brain.

1. Non-judgmentally: Just the Facts, Please!

Being non-judgmental means looking at things as they are, without labeling them as good or bad, right or wrong. It's like being a scientist observing an experiment – you're just collecting data, not deciding if the data is good or bad.

For neurodivergent teens, this skill can be super helpful:

- If you're autistic, you might sometimes feel judged for how you express yourself. Practicing non-judgment can help you accept yourself and others more easily.
- If you have ADHD, you might be hard on yourself for getting distracted. Non-judgment can help you notice distractions without beating yourself up about them.

Here's how to practice being non-judgmental:

1. Notice when you're making a judgment. Judgments often include words like "should," "good," "bad," "right," "wrong."
2. Separate the facts of the situation from your interpretations or opinions about it.
3. Describe the situation using just the facts.

Let's try a quick exercise:

Exercise 1: Fact vs. Judgment

For each pair of statements, identify which one is a fact (F) and which one is a judgment (J). Put the letter F in front of a fact, and the letter J in front of a judgment:

1. a) The temperature outside is 75°F.
   b) It's perfect weather for a picnic.

2. a) Sarah speaks three languages fluently.
   b) Sarah is really smart.

3. a) The concert lasted for two hours.
   b) The concert was too long.

(Answer key: 1. a) F, b) J; 2. a) F, b) J; 3. a) F, b) J)

Exercise 2: Spot the Judgment Words

Read the following sentences and underline any judgment words you can find:
a) You should always do your homework right after school.
b) The weather is nice today.
c) That movie was absolutely terrible.
d) I think blue is the best color.
e) There are five people in the room.

(Answer key: a) should, b) nice, c) terrible, d) best, e) No judgment words)

Great job! Remember, being non-judgmental doesn't mean you can't have opinions. It just means you're aware of the difference between facts and judgments.

2. One-mindfully: Full Focus Ahead!

Being one-mindful means giving your full attention to one thing at a time. It's like having a superpower that lets you zoom in on whatever you're doing right now.

For neurodivergent teens, one-mindfulness can be a game-changer:

- If you have ADHD, your mind might often feel scattered. One-mindfulness can help you focus on one task at a time.
- If you're autistic, you might sometimes feel overwhelmed by too much input. One-mindfulness can help you concentrate on one thing without getting overloaded.

Here's how to practice being one-mindful:

1. Choose one activity to focus on.
2. Give that activity your full attention.
3. When your mind wanders (and it will!), gently bring it back to the task at hand.

Let's try a one-mindful exercise:

Exercise 3: One-Mindful Eating

You'll need a small piece of food for this exercise (like a raisin, a piece of chocolate, or a small fruit).

1. Hold the food in your hand. Focus all your attention on it.
2. Look at it closely. Notice its color, shape, and texture.
3. Feel its weight in your hand. Is it smooth or rough?
4. Smell the food. What does it remind you of?
5. Slowly put the food in your mouth, but don't chew yet. Notice how it feels on your tongue.

6. Bite into the food. Pay attention to the taste and texture as you chew.
7. Swallow the food, noticing the sensation as it goes down.

In the space below, write about your experience. What did you notice that you might not usually pay attention to when eating?

Awesome job!

Real-Life Applications of "How" Skills

You might be wondering, "Okay, but how does this help me in real life?" Great question! Let's look at some examples:

1. Dealing with Sensory Overload:
When you're feeling overwhelmed by sensory input, you can use the non-judgmental skill to notice the sensations without labeling them as "bad." Then, you can one-mindfully focus on a calming sensory experience, like the feeling of a soft blanket.

2. Handling School Stress:
If you're stressed about a big project, you can use the effective skill to break it down into manageable steps and focus on what you can do, rather than worrying about the whole thing at once.

3. Navigating Social Situations:
When you're in a social situation that feels confusing, you can non-judgmentally observe what's happening, one-mindfully focus on the conversation, and effectively use the social skills that work best for you.

4. Managing ADHD Symptoms:
If you have ADHD and you notice you're having trouble focusing, you can non-judgmentally observe your distraction, one-mindfully bring your attention back to your task, and effectively use strategies that help you concentrate.

5. Coping with Change:
When faced with unexpected changes (which can be especially challenging for autistic individuals), you can non-judgmentally notice your reaction, one-mindfully focus on the present moment, and effectively use coping strategies that work for you.

Making "How" Skills Work for Your Neurodivergent Brain

Now, I know these skills might sound simple, but they can be challenging, especially for neurodivergent brains. Here are some tips to make them work better for you:

1. Start Small: Don't try to be non-judgmental, one-mindful, and effective all the time. Start with short periods or specific situations.

2. Use Visual Reminders: Create a symbol or use a specific color to remind you of each "How" skill. For example, you could wear a blue bracelet to remind you to be non-judgmental.

3. Incorporate Your Interests: If you have a special interest, use it to practice these skills. For example, if you love astronomy, you could practice one-mindful star-gazing.

4. Be Patient with Yourself: Your mind will make judgments, get distracted, and sometimes do things that aren't effective. That's okay! The goal is to notice these things, not to be perfect.

5. Adapt for Your Needs: If traditional mindfulness practices don't work for you, it's okay to modify them. For example, if sitting still is hard, you could practice one-mindful walking instead.

How" Skills in Action

Over the next week, try to practice each "How" skill at least once. Use the chart below to track your practice:

Day	Which "How" skill did I practice?	What situation did I use it in?	How did it go?
Monday			
Tuesday			
Wednesday			
Thursday			
Friday			
Saturday			
Sunday			

Chapter 2.3

Mindfulness and Sensory Experiences

In this section, we're going to consider how mindfulness can help you navigate the wild world of sensory input. Don't worry if you're not sure what mindfulness is yet – we'll break it down in a way that makes sense for your neurodivergent brain.

What's the Deal with Sensory Experiences?

First things first: let's talk about what we mean by "sensory experiences." These are basically all the things you can feel, see, hear, smell, and taste. For many neurodivergent folks, these experiences can be more intense or noticeable than they are for neurotypical people.

Here's a quick rundown of the main senses:

1. Sight (visual)
2. Sound (auditory)
3. Touch (tactile)
4. Smell (olfactory)
5. Taste (gustatory)
6. Body awareness (proprioception)
7. Balance and movement (vestibular)

You might find that some of these senses are extra sensitive for you, while others might not bother you much at all. That's totally normal! Everyone's sensory profile is different.

For neurodivergent brains, mindfulness can be super helpful when it comes to dealing with sensory stuff. Here's why:

1. It helps you notice what's going on in your body and environment.
2. It gives you a chance to pause before reacting to sensory input.
3. It can make overwhelming experiences feel more manageable.

Understanding Your Sensory Preferences

Everyone has different sensory likes and dislikes. Some neurodivergent folks might love the feeling of heavy blankets, while others can't stand them. Some might enjoy loud music, while others find it overwhelming.

Let's take a moment to explore your own sensory preferences:

1. Think about a sensory experience you really enjoy. Maybe it's the soft texture of your favorite sweater, the smell of freshly baked cookies, or the sound of rain on the roof.

Write down the sensory experience here:

What do you like about this experience? How does it make you feel?

2. Now, think about a sensory experience that you find challenging or overwhelming. It could be bright fluorescent lights, scratchy clothing tags, or the sound of people chewing.

Write down the sensory experience here:

What about this experience is difficult for you? How does it affect you?

Understanding your sensory preferences can help you make choices that support your well-being. It's also great info to share with friends, family, or teachers who want to support you better.

Mindful Strategies for Sensory Challenges

Now that we've practiced tuning into our senses and identified some of our preferences, let's talk about how mindfulness can help when sensory experiences get overwhelming.

The STOP Technique

When you're feeling overloaded by sensory input, try using the STOP technique:

S - Stop what you're doing
T - Take a breath
O - Observe what's happening in your body and mind
P - Proceed mindfully

Let's break this down:

1. Stop: Pause whatever you're doing. This gives your brain a chance to reset.

2. Take a breath: Take a slow, deep breath. This helps calm your nervous system.

3. Observe: Notice what's going on. Ask yourself:
   - What sensory input is bothering me?
   - How does my body feel? (Tense, shaky, hot?)
   - What thoughts are running through my mind?

4. Proceed: Based on what you observed, choose how to move forward. This might mean:
   - Removing yourself from the situation if possible
   - Using a coping strategy (like noise-canceling headphones or a fidget toy)
   - Asking for help or accommodation.

Putting It All Together: Mindful Sensory Awareness

Alright, now let's get into the good stuff – how to use mindfulness to work with your sensory experiences.

Exercise: The Sensory Check-In

This exercise is all about tuning into your senses, one at a time. You can do this anywhere, anytime.

1. Find a comfortable spot to sit or lie down.
2. Take a few deep breaths to settle in.
3. Now, we'll go through each sense:

- Sight: Look around and notice 5 things you can see. What colors, shapes, or textures do you observe?
- Sound: Listen carefully and identify 4 sounds you can hear. Are they loud or soft? Near or far?
- Touch: Pay attention to 3 things you can feel. Maybe it's the texture of your clothes, the temperature of the air, or the surface you're sitting on.
- Smell: Try to notice 2 scents in your environment. Don't worry if you can't smell anything – just notice that too!
- Taste: See if you can identify 1 taste in your mouth. Even if you haven't eaten recently, there might be a subtle flavor there.

4. Take a moment to jot down what you noticed for each sense in the space below:

Touch:

Sight:

Smell:

Sound:

Taste:

Sensory Pleasure Scavenger Hunt

Over the next week, try to notice and document sensory experiences that bring you joy or comfort. They don't have to be big things – even small pleasures count!

Here are some examples to get you started:

- The satisfying click of a keyboard
- The cool side of the pillow
- The smell of your favorite food cooking
- The feeling of warm sunlight on your skin
- The sight of your favorite color

Your Sensory Joy List

Chapter 2.4

Mindful Stimming Practices

Let's talk about what stimming is. Stimming, short for self-stimulatory behavior, is basically any repetitive movement or sound that you do to help regulate your sensory input or emotions. It's super common for neurodivergent folks, especially those with autism or ADHD.

Some examples of stimming include:
- Flapping your hands
- Rocking back and forth
- Twirling your hair
- Tapping your fingers
- Repeating words or phrases
- Fidgeting with objects

Here's the thing: stimming is totally normal and healthy. It's your brain's way of dealing with sensory overload, managing emotions, or just feeling good. So if anyone's ever told you to stop stimming, you can politely let them know that it's actually really important for your well-being.

Mindfulness and Stimming: A Perfect Match

Now, you might be wondering, "What does mindfulness have to do with stimming?" Great question! Mindfulness is all about paying attention to the present moment without judgment. When you combine mindfulness with stimming, you can:

1. Become more aware of when and why you stim
2. Enhance the positive effects of stimming
3. Discover new stims that work well for you
4. Use stimming as a tool for emotional regulation.

Sounds pretty cool, right? Let's engage in some mindful stimming practices!

Technique 1: Stim Breathing

This technique combines stimming with mindful breathing. It's great for calming down or centering yourself.

1. Choose a stim that has a rhythm to it (like rocking or finger tapping).
2. Sync your breathing with your stim:
   - Inhale for one repetition of the stim
   - Exhale for one repetition of the stim
3. Focus on the sensation of your breath and the rhythm of your stim.
4. Continue for 5-10 breaths, or longer if it feels good.

How did that feel? Did syncing your breath with your stim change the experience? Write your thoughts here in your workbook:

Technique 2: The Stim Scan

This technique is all about really tuning into your stim while you're doing it. Here's how:

1. Choose a stim you'd like to focus on.
2. Get into a comfortable position and start your stim.
3. Close your eyes if that feels okay.
4. As you stim, pay attention to:

-The physical sensations in your body
- Any sounds associated with the stim
- How your emotions shift as you stim
5. If your mind wanders, gently bring your attention back to the stim.
6. Continue for as long as it feels good to you.

After you're done, take a moment to reflect.

Write your observations here:

How did it feel to focus so closely on your stim?

Did you notice anything new about this stim?

How do you feel now compared to before you started?

Stimming in Different Situations

Now that we've practiced some mindful stimming techniques, let's talk about how to use them in different situations.

At School or Work

Sometimes, you might need to stim in places where you don't want to draw too much attention. Here are some ideas for subtle stims:

- Use a fidget toy under your desk
- Doodle or trace patterns on paper
- Tap your toes inside your shoes
- Chew gum or suck on a hard candy
- Use a stretchy bracelet to play with

Remember, it's okay to take breaks if you need to stim more actively. You could excuse yourself to the bathroom or find a quiet corner during lunch.

In Social Situations

Stimming in social situations can sometimes feel tricky. Here are some tips:

1. Be open about your needs: Let friends know that stimming helps you feel comfortable.
2. Choose less noticeable stims if you're feeling self-conscious.
3. Use mindful breathing or visualization if you need a break.
4. Remember that true friends will accept you as you are, stims and all!

When You're Stressed

Stimming can be super helpful when you're feeling overwhelmed or anxious. Here's a mindful approach:

1. Notice that you're feeling stressed (your Stim Awareness Journal can help with this).
2. Choose a calming stim from your toolkit.

3. Find a comfortable spot if possible.
4. Use the Stim Scan technique to really focus on your stim.
5. Continue until you feel more relaxed.

Exercise: My Stimming Plan

Let's create a plan for using mindful stimming in different situations. Fill in the blanks:

My Stimming Plan	
When I'm at school, I can stim by:	
In social situations, I'm comfortable stimming by:	
When I'm feeling stressed, my go-to stim is:	
My favorite mindful stimming technique is:	
If someone asks about my stimming, I can say:	

Wrapping It Up

Wow, we've covered a lot about mindful stimming! Let's recap the main points:

1. Stimming is a normal, healthy behavior that helps you regulate.
2. Mindfulness can enhance your stimming practices.
3. Understanding your stims helps you use them more effectively.
4. There are lots of ways to stim mindfully in different situations.
5. Accepting your stims is an important part of self-acceptance.

Remember, mindful stimming is a skill that takes practice. Be patient with yourself as you explore these techniques. Some days will be easier than others, and that's totally okay.

Keep stimming, keep being mindful, and most importantly, keep being your awesome neurodivergent self!

Stim Awareness Journal

For this exercise, we're going to start paying more attention to your stimming habits. Grab a notebook or use the space below to create a Stim Awareness Journal. For the next week, try to notice when you stim and jot down some notes about it.

Here's what to track:

1. What kind of stim did you do?
2. When did you do it?
3. What was happening around you?
4. How were you feeling before, during, and after?

Here's a template you can use:

Stim Awareness Journal

Date:..

Stim Type

Time

Situation

Feelings before

Feelings during

Feelings after

Stim Awareness Journal

Date:..

Stim Type

Time

Situation

Feelings before

Feelings during

Feelings after

Chapter 2.5

DBT Mindfulness Exercises for Neurodivergent Teens

If you've made it this far, you're probably starting to get the hang of what mindfulness is all about. But maybe you're wondering, "How do I actually do this mindfulness thing, especially when my brain works a little differently?" This section is all about practical DBT mindfulness exercises that are tailor-made for neurodivergent teens like you.

Why Mindfulness Matters for Neurodivergent Brains

Before we dive into the exercises, let's talk about why mindfulness is such a big deal for neurodivergent folks. If you're autistic or have ADHD, your brain might process information and experiences in unique ways. This can be super cool, but it can also sometimes feel overwhelming or confusing.

Mindfulness can help you:
1. Slow down racing thoughts
2. Manage sensory overload
3. Improve focus and concentration
4. Understand and regulate your emotions better
5. Feel more grounded in your body and the present moment

The best part? There's no one "right" way to do mindfulness. We're going to explore a bunch of different exercises, and you can pick and choose the ones that work best for your brain.

Getting Started: The Mindfulness Mindset

Before we jump into the exercises, let's talk about the mindset that can help make mindfulness work for you:

1. Curiosity: Approach each exercise with an open, curious mind. It's all about exploring your experiences, not judging them.

2. Patience: Mindfulness is a skill, and like any skill, it takes practice. Be patient with yourself as you learn.

3. Non-judgment: Try not to label your thoughts or experiences as "good" or "bad." They just are what they are.

4. Beginners Mind: Even if you've tried mindfulness before, approach each practice like it's brand new. You might notice something you never did before!

5. Gentleness: Be kind to yourself. If your mind wanders (and it will), gently bring it back to the present moment.

Mindful Music Listening

For this exercise, we're going to use music to practice mindfulness. This can be especially great if you're someone who really connects with music.

What you'll need:
- A piece of music (any kind you like)
- Headphones (if you prefer)
- A quiet space

Steps:
1. Choose a song you like, but try to pick one you haven't listened to in a while.
2. Get comfortable and put on your headphones if you're using them.
3. Close your eyes if that feels okay.
4. Press play and really listen to the music. Notice:
   - The different instruments
   - The rhythm and beat
   - The lyrics (if there are any)
   - How the music makes your body feel
   - Any emotions that come up

5. If your mind wanders, gently bring it back to the music.
6. Listen to the whole song this way.

After the song ends, take a moment to reflect:

What did you notice that you've never noticed before?

How did your body feel during the song?

What emotions came up?

The Mindful Doodle

This exercise combines mindfulness with creativity, which can be really fun for neurodivergent brains

Steps:
1. Set a timer for 5 minutes.
2. Start drawing whatever comes to mind. It doesn't have to be anything specific or "good."
3. As you draw, pay attention to:
   - The sensation of the pen or pencil on the paper
   - The shapes and lines you're creating
   - Any thoughts or feelings that come up as you draw
4. If your mind wanders, gently bring it back to the act of drawing.
5. When the timer goes off, stop drawing.

Doodle Here

Take a look at your doodle. What do you notice?

How did it feel to draw mindfully?

Pro tip: You can do this exercise anytime you need a quick mindfulness break. It's great for when you're feeling restless or need to refocus.

CHAPTER 3
Distress Tolerance Skills

Chapter 3.1

Crisis Survival Strategies for Meltdowns and Overwhelm

In this section, we're going to talk about crisis survival strategies that can help you when you're feeling like you're at your breaking point.

Understanding Meltdowns and Overwhelm

First things first, let's talk about what a meltdown or overwhelm looks like. If you're neurodivergent, you probably know this feeling all too well. It's when your brain gets so overloaded that it feels like you can't take it anymore.

Meltdowns can look like crying, yelling, or needing to escape a situation. It might feel like you've lost control and everything is just too much. Shutdowns, on the other hand, might be when you go quiet, withdraw from everyone, and feel like you can't respond or think clearly.

Why Do Meltdowns Happen?

Meltdowns happen when you're pushed past your limits. It could be sensory overload—like too much noise, light, or chaos. Or it could be emotional overload—like feeling stressed out, anxious, or frustrated. Sometimes, it's a mix of both.

Imagine your brain as a cup. Throughout the day, drops of water (or stress) fill your cup. Usually, you can handle it, but if too many drops fill up too quickly, the cup overflows. That overflow is your meltdown or shutdown.

Crisis Survival Strategies

So, what can you do when you feel like you're about to hit that overflow point? That's where these crisis survival strategies come in. Think of them as your emergency toolkit, filled with things you can do to help calm your mind and body until the storm passes.

1. Grounding Techniques: Find Your Anchor

Grounding techniques help you stay connected to the present moment when everything feels like it's slipping away. It's like throwing down an anchor to stop the waves from tossing you around.

Box Breathing

This technique is called "box breathing" because you breathe in a pattern that's shaped like a box—four counts in, four counts hold, four counts out, four counts hold.

- Step 1: Inhale through your nose for a count of four. Feel the air filling your lungs, expanding your chest and belly.
- Step 2: Hold your breath for a count of four. Notice the stillness in your body as you hold the breath.
- Step 3: Exhale slowly through your mouth for a count of four. Imagine you're letting go of any stress or tension as the air leaves your body.
- Step 4: Hold your breath for a count of four before starting the next inhale. This completes one "box."

Repeat this for a few cycles until you start to feel calmer. Use the following prompts to reflect:

Describe how you felt before starting the box breathing exercise.
Were you tense, anxious, or overwhelmed? How did these feelings show up in your body?

How easy or difficult was it to focus on your breath?
Did your mind wander? If so, how did you bring your focus back to your breathing?

How do you feel now, after practicing box breathing?
Note any changes in your physical or emotional state. Do you feel more relaxed, centered, or calm?

In what situations do you think box breathing would be most helpful for you?

3. Sensory Soothing: Calm Your Senses

If sensory overload is triggering your meltdown, calming your senses can be a lifesaver. This is all about finding sensory inputs that soothe you instead of overwhelm you.

Sensory Kit Creation

Create a sensory kit that you can use when you feel a meltdown coming on. Your kit can include:

- A soft blanket or piece of fabric to touch.
- Noise-canceling headphones or soothing music.
- A small object with a pleasant smell, like lavender oil.
- A favorite snack that tastes comforting.

Step-by-Step Guide to Creating Your Sensory Kit:

1. Identify your calming sensory inputs.
   Think about what textures, sounds, smells, and tastes help you feel calm. Write them down:

Gather items that match your calming inputs.

List the items you want to include in your sensory kit. Make sure they're easy to carry or store in a small bag or box.

Reflect on your experience using the kit.

The next time you use your sensory kit, note how it made you feel. Did certain items work better than others? Would you add or remove anything?

Plan when and where to use your kit.

Think about situations where you might need your sensory kit. It could be in crowded places, before a stressful event, or during moments of overwhelm. Write down when you plan to use it:

Chapter 3.2

ACCEPTS: Activities, Contributing, Comparisons, Emotions, Pushing Away, Thoughts, Sensations

When life throws curveballs, especially for teens with neurodivergent minds, it's easy to feel overwhelmed and stressed. These moments can make it hard to think clearly or find a way out of the discomfort. That's where the ACCEPTS skills come in. ACCEPTS is a set of tools designed to help you tolerate distress in healthy ways when your emotions are running high.

ACCEPTS stands for Activities, Contributing, Comparisons, Emotions, Pushing Away, Thoughts, and Sensations. Each of these tools offers a different way to cope with distress, giving you options when you need them most. Let's break down each component of ACCEPTS and explore how you can use these strategies to manage overwhelming situations.

1. Activities: Shifting Your Focus

When you're overwhelmed, sometimes the best thing you can do is to distract yourself with an activity. Engaging in something you enjoy or something that requires your full attention can help take your mind off what's bothering you. This gives your emotions time to settle down before you face the situation again.

Examples of Activities:
- Physical Exercise: Go for a run, dance to your favorite songs, or take a yoga class. Moving your body can help release built-up stress and improve your mood.

- Creative Arts: Draw, paint, write, or engage in any form of creative expression. Art allows you to channel your emotions into something tangible, giving you a sense of accomplishment.
- Gaming: Play a video game that requires focus and strategy. Immersing yourself in a game can be a great way to distract your mind.
- Puzzles and Brain Teasers: Try solving a puzzle, playing Sudoku, or working on a crossword. These activities engage your brain and keep you busy.

My Activity

Make a list of activities that you enjoy or that help you calm down when you're feeling stressed. Writem them in the spaces below.

Choose one activity from your list and try it the next time you feel overwhelmed. Afterward, write down how it made you feel.

Date:..

Activity

____

____

How I felt before the activity

____

____

____

How I felt after the activity

____

____

____

Choose one activity from your list and try it the next time you feel overwhelmed. Afterward, write down how it made you feel.

Date:...

Activity

How I felt before the activity

How I felt after the activity

---

2. Contributing: Doing Something for Others

Helping others can be a powerful way to lift your own spirits. When you're focused on someone else's needs, it takes the attention off your own problems, even if just for a while. Plus, contributing to others' well-being can give you a sense of purpose and connection.

Examples of Contributing:
- Volunteering: Help out at a local charity, animal shelter, or community event.
- Random Acts of Kindness: Hold the door for someone, pay a compliment, or help a friend with their homework.
- Chores at Home: Offer to do extra chores around the house, like cooking dinner or cleaning up. It's a simple way to contribute to your family's well-being.
- Support a Friend: Listen to a friend who's going through a tough time, offer advice, or just be there for them.

3. Comparisons: Gaining Perspective

When you're feeling low, comparing yourself to others who have overcome similar challenges or thinking about times when you've handled tough situations can help you gain perspective. It's not about minimizing your feelings but about recognizing your resilience and ability to get through hard times.

Examples of Comparisons:
- Reflect on Past Successes: Think about a time when you faced a difficult situation and managed to get through it. What did you do that worked? How can you apply that to your current situation?
- Compare to a Less Ideal Situation: Consider how things could be worse, not to diminish your struggles, but to remind yourself of the strengths and resources you have.
- Look to Role Models: Think about someone you admire who has faced challenges. What did they do to overcome their obstacles? How can their experience inspire you?

Positive Comparisons

Identify a past situation where you successfully navigated a difficult moment. Reflect on what helped you during that time and how you can use those strategies now.

What was the challenge?

What did I do to overcome it?

How can I apply this experience to my current situation?

Write about a role model who has inspired you. What challenges did they face, and what did you learn from their journey?

Who is my role model?

What challenges did they face?

What did I learn from their experience?

4. Emotions: Generating Positive Feelings

Sometimes, the best way to combat negative emotions is by actively creating positive ones. This doesn't mean ignoring your feelings, but rather balancing them out by doing things that make you feel good.

Examples of Generating Positive Emotions:
- Watch a Funny Movie: Laughter is a great way to lighten your mood and reduce stress.
- Listen to Uplifting Music: Play songs that make you feel happy or energetic. Music has the power to shift your mood in a matter of minutes.
- Look at Pictures that Make You Smile: Keep a collection of photos that bring back happy memories. Looking at them can bring a sense of joy and nostalgia.
- Practice Gratitude: Focus on the things in your life that you're thankful for. Gratitude can help shift your mindset from what's wrong to what's right.

5. Pushing Away: Setting Boundaries with Your Thoughts

When your mind is cluttered with distressing thoughts, sometimes the best strategy is to mentally push those thoughts away. This doesn't mean you're ignoring the problem—it just means you're giving yourself some space before you come back to it with a clearer head.

Examples of Pushing Away:
- Visualize a Box: Imagine putting your distressing thoughts in a box and closing the lid. Picture yourself setting the box aside on a shelf, knowing you can come back to it later.
- Mental Vacation: Take a mental break by imagining a peaceful place where you feel safe and relaxed. Spend a few minutes there in your mind.
- Set a Time Limit: If your thoughts keep coming back, set a timer for 10 minutes and allow yourself to worry during that time. When the timer goes off, push those thoughts away and move on to something else.

6. Thoughts: Reframing Your Mindset

The way you think about a situation can greatly impact how you feel. Sometimes, by changing your perspective or reframing your thoughts, you can reduce the intensity of your emotions.

Examples of Reframing Thoughts:
- Challenge Negative Thoughts: When you catch yourself thinking negatively, ask yourself if there's another way to look at the situation. For example, instead of thinking, "I'll never get this right," you might reframe it to, "I'm still learning, and it's okay to make mistakes."

- Use Affirmations: Replace negative thoughts with positive affirmations. For example, if you're feeling anxious about a social situation, you might tell yourself, "I'm capable, and I can handle this."

- Focus on Solutions: Instead of dwelling on what's wrong, shift your focus to what you can do to improve the situation. This doesn't mean ignoring the problem, but rather taking proactive steps to address it.

- Practice Self-Compassion: Be kind to yourself when things go wrong. Instead of criticizing yourself, think about how you would comfort a friend in the same situation, and offer yourself that same kindness.

7. Sensations: Using Physical Sensations to Distract and Calm

Engaging your senses can be a powerful way to distract yourself from distressing emotions. By focusing on sensory experiences, you can bring your attention to the present moment and away from overwhelming thoughts.

Examples of Sensations:
- Hold an Ice Cube: The cold sensation can snap you out of an intense emotional state by redirecting your focus to the physical feeling in your hand.
- Take a Cold Shower: The sudden change in temperature can help shift your focus and calm your nervous system.

Chapter 3.3:

Self-Soothing with the Five Senses

Whether it's the screeching sound of a blender or the bright lights of a classroom, sensory overload can be a real challenge. The good news? You have tools at your disposal to help soothe yourself. And guess what? They all start with the senses you already use every day.

Sensory Soothing: Why It Matters

Let's start with the basics: our senses—sight, sound, touch, smell, and taste—are like a constant stream of information coming at us. For many neurodivergent folks, this flow can sometimes feel overwhelming. That's where self-soothing with the five senses comes in. By intentionally engaging with your senses in a calming way, you can help reduce stress and bring yourself back to a more balanced place.

Using Your Senses to Self-Soothe

Sight (Visual Comfort)

Sometimes, bright lights or busy patterns can be too much. To soothe yourself visually, you might try:

- Soft Lighting: Switch to a lamp with a soft bulb or use a dimmer if you have one.
- Calming Colors: Surround yourself with colors you find relaxing. Think pastels or muted tones.
- Visual Breaks: Look at something that makes you happy, like a favorite photo or a calming scene from nature.

Sound (Auditory Comfort)

Noisy environments can be tough. To help with this, consider:

- Noise-Canceling Tools: Use headphones or earplugs to block out distracting sounds.
- Soothing Sounds: Play gentle music, white noise, or nature sounds that you find calming.
- Sound Breaks: Take breaks from noisy environments when you need to.

Touch (Tactile Comfort)

Touch can be incredibly soothing or irritating, depending on what you're feeling. Try:

- Comfortable Fabrics: Wear clothes made from soft, breathable fabrics that you enjoy.
- Weighted Items: Use a weighted blanket or a fidget toy for calming pressure.
- Soothing Textures: Touch something you find comforting, like a soft stuffed animal or a smooth stone.

Smell (Olfactory Comfort)

Scents can have a big impact on your mood and comfort. To manage this:

- Favorite Scents: Use essential oils or candles with scents you love, like lavender or vanilla.
- Avoid Overpowering Odors: Be mindful of strong smells that might bother you, like strong perfumes or cleaning products.
- Fresh Air: Open a window or step outside to get some fresh air if indoor smells are overwhelming.

Taste (Gustatory Comfort)

The taste and texture of food can either be a comfort or a challenge. To manage this:

- Comfort Foods: Choose foods with textures and flavors that you find comforting.
- Mindful Eating: Focus on eating slowly and enjoying each bite.
- Hydration: Drink water or other soothing beverages to keep your mouth and throat comfortable.

Visual Comfort Checklist

Find Your Safe Spot: Choose a place where you feel visually comfortable.

Add Visual Comfort: Use soft lighting or calming colors.

Write down what visual strategies worked for you and how they made you feel.

Auditory Comfort Toolkit

What sounds bother you the most?

List the tools and strategies you use to manage these sounds.

How well do these strategies help? What might you adjust?

Chapter 3.4:

IMPROVE the Moment

This is a super important part of your distress tolerance toolkit: "IMPROVE the Moment." This skill is all about making tough situations more bearable. When you're feeling overwhelmed, upset, or just plain stuck, these strategies can help you shift your mindset, feel a bit better, and keep going.

What is IMPROVE the Moment?

"IMPROVE" is an acronym that stands for:

- Imagery
- Meaning
- Prayer
- Relaxation
- One Thing in the Moment
- Vacation
- Encouragement

Each of these skills offers a different way to make a difficult moment more manageable. Let's break them down and see how you can use each one to your advantage.

I - Imagery: Picture Your Safe Place

Imagery is like a mental vacation. It's all about using your imagination to create a scene in your mind where you feel safe, calm, and in control. This can be especially helpful if you're feeling anxious, overwhelmed, or trapped.

How to Use Imagery:

1. Close your eyes (if you're comfortable doing so) and take a deep breath.
2. Picture a place where you feel completely safe and relaxed. This could be a real place, like your bedroom or a quiet park, or an imaginary one, like a peaceful beach or a cozy forest cabin.
3. Focus on the details. What does the air smell like? What sounds do you hear? What do you see around you?
4. Imagine yourself in this place, feeling calm and at ease. Stay there in your mind for a few minutes, just soaking in the peace.

Take a few minutes to create your own safe place in your mind. Use the prompts below to guide you.

Where is your safe place?

What do you see around you?

What sounds can you hear?

What smells or scents are in the air?

How does this place make you feel?

Whenever you're feeling stressed or overwhelmed, remember you can visit this safe place in your mind.

M - Meaning: Finding Purpose in the Pain

When things get tough, finding meaning in the situation can help you cope. This doesn't mean everything happens for a reason, but rather that you can choose to create your own meaning or purpose, even in difficult times.

How to Find Meaning:
1. Reflect on the situation. What's happening right now that's causing you distress?
2. Think about what this situation might be teaching you. Are there any lessons to learn?
3. Consider how you can use this experience to grow stronger or more resilient.
4. If it's hard to find meaning, think about what you can do with this experience. Can you use it to help others or yourself in the future?

Think about a recent difficult experience. Use the questions below to find meaning in it.

What happened?

What did you learn from this experience?

How might this experience help you in the future?

Remember, you have the power to create meaning in your life, even during the toughest times.

P - Prayer: Connecting to Something Greater

Prayer in DBT isn't necessarily about religion; it's about connecting with something greater than yourself. This could be a higher power, the universe, nature, or even just a deep sense of inner peace. It's about reaching out for strength and guidance when you're feeling lost or overwhelmed.

How to Use Prayer:
1. Think about what you believe in, whether it's a higher power, the universe, or your inner strength.
2. Reach out to that source of strength. This could be through traditional prayer, a silent meditation, or simply talking to yourself or the universe.
3. Ask for the help, strength, or guidance you need in this moment.
4. Focus on the feeling of connection and let it bring you comfort.

Take a moment to create your own prayer or meditation. Use the space below to write down what you might say or think when using this skill.

Who or what are you reaching out to?

What do you ask for?

How does this connection make you feel?

Use this prayer or meditation whenever you need a moment of peace or guidance.

Think about a recent difficult experience. Use the questions below to find meaning in it.

What happened?

What did you learn from this experience?

How might this experience help you in the future?

Remember, you have the power to create meaning in your life, even during the toughest times.

P - Prayer: Connecting to Something Greater

Prayer in DBT isn't necessarily about religion; it's about connecting with something greater than yourself. This could be a higher power, the universe, nature, or even just a deep sense of inner peace. It's about reaching out for strength and guidance when you're feeling lost or overwhelmed.

R - Relaxation: Letting Go of Tension

Relaxation is about consciously releasing the tension in your body and mind. This can be especially helpful if you're feeling anxious, tense, or on edge.

How to Relax:
1. Find a comfortable place to sit or lie down.
2. Take a few deep breaths, in through your nose and out through your mouth.
3. Starting with your feet, tense the muscles as tightly as you can, then release. Move up your body, doing this with each muscle group (legs, stomach, arms, shoulders, face).
4. As you relax each muscle group, imagine the tension leaving your body.
5. Once you've relaxed your whole body, take a few more deep breaths, letting go of any remaining tension.

Relaxation is a skill you can use anytime you're feeling tense or stressed. It's a great way to calm your body and mind.

O - One Thing in the Moment: Stay Grounded

When you're overwhelmed, it can feel like everything is happening all at once. Focusing on one thing in the moment can help you stay grounded and present.

How to Practice One Thing in the Moment:
1. Choose one task or activity to focus on.
2. Give your full attention to that task. If your mind wanders, gently bring it back to the task.
3. If you're struggling, you can also focus on your breathing or on a physical sensation, like the feeling of your feet on the ground.
4. Keep bringing your mind back to the present moment, even if it keeps wandering.

V - Vacation: Take a Break

Sometimes, you just need a break. Taking a mental or physical "vacation" can help you recharge and come back to the situation with a clearer mind.

How to Take a Vacation:
1. If you can, take a short break from the situation that's causing you distress. This might be a walk outside, a few minutes of listening to music, or even a quick nap.
2. If you can't physically leave the situation, take a mental vacation. Imagine yourself in a place where you feel relaxed and happy.
3. Use this time to recharge and come back to the situation with renewed energy.

E - Encouragement: Be Your Own Cheerleader

Encouragement is all about self-compassion and positive self-talk. When you're feeling down, stressed, or overwhelmed, it's important to be kind to yourself.

How to Encourage Yourself:
1. Acknowledge what you're going through. It's okay to feel upset or stressed.
2. Remind yourself of your strengths and past successes.
3. Talk to yourself the way you would talk to a friend who's going through a tough time.
4. Use positive affirmations or mantras that resonate with you.

Chapter 3.5:

Radical Acceptance for Neurodivergent Experiences

Now, you might be wondering, "What's so radical about acceptance?" Great question! Radical acceptance is more than just saying, "Okay, fine," to something you don't like. It's about fully and completely acknowledging reality as it is—without trying to fight it, change it, or wish it were different. It's saying, "This is the way it is right now," even when it's hard.

For neurodivergent teens like you, radical acceptance can be a superpower. Life throws a lot at you—sometimes things that feel unfair, overwhelming, or just plain confusing. Radical acceptance doesn't mean giving up or liking everything that happens. Instead, it's about freeing yourself from the struggle against reality. This acceptance can help you find peace, even in tough situations, and it's a powerful tool for reducing emotional suffering.

Why Radical Acceptance Matters

Before we jump into how to practice radical acceptance, let's talk about why it's so important, especially for neurodivergent teens.

1. Life is Full of Unavoidable Challenges: We all face things we can't control, like how other people treat us, unexpected changes, or the way our brains work. Trying to fight these realities can lead to more pain and frustration.

2. Reduces Emotional Suffering: When we refuse to accept reality, we often make things harder for ourselves. For example, if you keep wishing your ADHD didn't make school so tough, you might end up feeling even more frustrated and discouraged.

Radical acceptance helps you stop adding extra layers of suffering on top of the challenges you're already facing.

3. Creates Room for Change: It might sound strange, but accepting things as they are can actually open up space for change. When you stop fighting reality, you free up mental and emotional energy to focus on what you can do.

4. Builds Resilience: Practicing radical acceptance strengthens your ability to cope with life's ups and downs. It's like building a mental muscle that helps you handle difficult situations without getting knocked down.

Radical Acceptance and Neurodivergence: A Perfect Match

Radical acceptance is especially useful for neurodivergent teens because your experiences are often different from those of your neurotypical peers. Society might not always understand or accommodate your needs, and that can be tough. But radical acceptance can help you navigate these challenges in a healthier, more balanced way.

1. Accepting Your Neurodivergent Brain:

Your brain is wired differently, and that's okay. Radical acceptance means recognizing and embracing your neurodivergence without judgment. Whether you're autistic, have ADHD, or live with other neurodivergent traits, radical acceptance allows you to see your unique brain as part of who you are, rather than something that needs fixing.

2. Navigating Social Expectations:

Social situations can be tricky for neurodivergent teens. Maybe you struggle with understanding social cues, or maybe you find it hard to focus in loud environments. Radical acceptance helps you acknowledge these challenges without beating yourself up. It's about saying, "This is hard for me, and that's okay. I'm doing my best."

How to Practice Radical Acceptance

Now that we know why radical acceptance is important, let's talk about how to actually do it. Radical acceptance isn't something you do just once—it's a practice, something you work on over time. Here are some steps and tips to help you get started.

Step 1: Recognize What You're Resisting

The first step in practicing radical acceptance is to notice when you're resisting reality. This resistance might show up as thoughts like, "This isn't fair," "Why me?" or "I wish things were different." Pay attention to the situations that trigger these thoughts.

Think about a recent situation that made you feel frustrated, angry, or sad. In the space below, write down what happened and the thoughts you had about it. Then, circle any thoughts that show resistance to reality (e.g., "This shouldn't be happening," "I wish I didn't have to deal with this").

Situation

Thoughts

Step 2: Acknowledge Reality

Once you've identified your resistance, the next step is to acknowledge reality. This doesn't mean you have to like what's happening—it just means you recognize it as it is. You might say to yourself, "This is the way things are right now," or "This is what's happening, and I can't change it in this moment."

Using the situation you wrote about in the last exercise, practice acknowledging reality. In the space below, write a statement that reflects your acceptance of the situation.

Acknowledgment

Step 3: Let Go of the Fight

After acknowledging reality, the next step is to let go of the struggle against it. This is where radical acceptance really comes into play. Letting go doesn't mean you're giving up or that you approve of what's happening. It just means you're choosing not to waste energy on fighting something you can't change.

Think about the situation you've been working on in the previous exercises. Imagine letting go of the need to change or resist it. What would it feel like to stop fighting against reality? In the space on the next page, describe how you would feel if you let go.

Letting Go

Step 4: Focus on What You Can Control

Radical acceptance isn't about being passive or giving up—it's about recognizing what you can and can't control. Once you've accepted a situation, you can focus on what you *can* do. This might mean changing your perspective, finding ways to cope, or taking action in areas where you have influence.

For the situation you've been working on, think about what you can control. What actions can you take to cope or improve the situation? Write down your ideas below.

Actions I Can Take

CHAPTER 4
Emotion Regulation Skills

Chapter 4.1:

Identifying and Labeling Emotions

Emotions are powerful. They can lift you up, weigh you down, or even leave you feeling confused. For many teens, especially those with neurodivergent minds, emotions can sometimes feel like a whirlwind—one moment you're calm, and the next, you're overwhelmed by a wave of feelings. Understanding your emotions is the first step in gaining control over them.

When you can identify and label your emotions, you take away some of their power. Instead of letting your emotions run the show, you get to decide how to respond. This chapter is all about helping you recognize what you're feeling and giving those feelings a name. Once you can do that, you'll find it easier to manage your emotions, communicate with others, and make decisions that feel right for you.

The Importance of Naming Your Emotions

Imagine you're in a dark room, feeling around for something that's making you uncomfortable. You can't see it, so it's hard to know what to do about it. But as soon as you turn on the light and see what it is, you can figure out how to handle it. That's what it's like when you name your emotions.

When you don't know what you're feeling, it's like being in that dark room. Your emotions might feel big and scary, and you might react in ways that don't actually help the situation. But when you can name your emotion—whether it's anger, sadness, joy, or anxiety—you can start to understand why you're feeling that way and what you can do about it.

Think of emotions like colors. If you didn't know the names of different colors, you might struggle to describe what you see. The same goes for emotions—if you don't have the right words, it's hard to describe what you're feeling, even to yourself.

Common Emotions and Their Triggers

To get better at identifying your emotions, it helps to start with the basics. Here are some common emotions and what might trigger them:

1. Anger– Often triggered by feeling hurt, frustrated, or treated unfairly. It's a natural response when something or someone crosses your boundaries.
2. Sadness – Can arise from loss, disappointment, or feeling disconnected. Sadness is a signal that something important to you is missing.
3. Fear – Triggered by danger, uncertainty, or the unknown. Fear can help protect you, but it can also hold you back if it becomes overwhelming.
4. Joy – Brought on by positive experiences, achieving something, or connecting with others. Joy is a reminder of the good things in life.
5. Anxiety– Often comes from worry about the future or feeling out of control. Anxiety can be a motivator, but too much of it can be paralyzing.
6. Surprise – Triggered by something unexpected, whether it's good or bad. Surprise can lead to a mix of emotions depending on what the situation is.

Take a moment to think about what usually triggers your emotions. Write down a list of common situations that bring up these feelings for you.

Anger Triggers

Sadness Triggers

Fear Triggers

Joy Triggers

Anxiety Triggers

The Spectrum of Emotions: Moving Beyond Basic Labels

While it's useful to start with basic emotions, human feelings are often more complex. Think of emotions as existing on a spectrum—where anger can range from mild irritation to full-blown rage, and sadness can range from feeling a little blue to deep grief.

Imagine a rainbow of emotions. Each color represents a different feeling, and just like there are shades of each color, there are shades of each emotion. Understanding these shades can help you get more specific about what you're feeling.

Labeling Your Emotions: Why It's Worth the Effort

Once you've identified your emotion, the next step is to label it. Labeling means putting your feelings into words, which can make them feel less overwhelming and more manageable.

Studies show that when people label their emotions, they experience a decrease in emotional intensity. It's as if by naming the emotion, you're taking a step back from it, which allows you to think more clearly and make better decisions.

Think of labeling emotions like organizing a cluttered room. When everything is scattered around, it's hard to know where to start. But once you start labeling and organizing, the mess doesn't seem so overwhelming anymore.

Identifying and labeling your emotions is a lifelong skill. It's not always easy, and sometimes it might feel like you're getting it wrong. But that's okay. The more you practice, the better you'll get at understanding your emotional landscape.

Remember, your emotions are a part of you, but they don't have to control you. By learning to identify and label them, you're taking the first step toward mastering them. And with the DBT skills you'll continue to learn, you'll have the tools you need to handle whatever emotions come your way.

Chapter 4.2:

Understanding Emotional Vulnerability and Neurodivergence

Emotional vulnerability is a term you might have heard before, but it can feel a little fuzzy to understand. Simply put, emotional vulnerability refers to how sensitive we are to our emotions. For some, emotions are like gentle waves—easy to ride and predictable. For others, especially those who are neurodivergent, emotions can feel like crashing tides, powerful and overwhelming. This chapter will help you explore what emotional vulnerability means for you, especially in the context of being neurodivergent.

What is Emotional Vulnerability?

Think of emotional vulnerability as your emotional "radar." Some people's radars are set to a low frequency, meaning they only pick up on big, obvious signals. Others have radars that pick up even the tiniest emotional signals, which can make the world feel intense. When your radar is highly sensitive, you might find that small things others might brush off—like a change in someone's tone of voice or an unexpected event—can trigger a strong emotional response.

For neurodivergent teens, emotional vulnerability can be even more heightened. This heightened sensitivity isn't a flaw; it's simply a part of how your brain processes emotions. It's like having a superpower that lets you experience the world deeply and vividly. However, without the right tools, this superpower can sometimes feel more like a burden.

Imagine you're sitting in a room with a radar screen in front of you. For some people, the screen only lights up when something big happens—like an argument or a major life event.

But for you, the radar picks up everything: the slight change in a friend's mood, the pressure of a deadline, the way someone looked at you. All these signals light up your screen, making it hard to know which ones to focus on and which ones to ignore.

Why Are Neurodivergent Teens More Emotionally Vulnerable?

Neurodivergent teens, including those with Autism and ADHD, often have unique neurological wiring that can make emotional experiences more intense. Here's why:

1. Sensory Sensitivity: Many neurodivergent individuals have heightened sensory experiences. Sounds, lights, textures, and even smells can feel more intense, which can amplify emotional reactions. For instance, a loud noise might not just be startling—it could be overwhelming and lead to feelings of anxiety or anger.

2. Social Challenges: Navigating social situations can be more challenging, leading to misunderstandings or feelings of rejection. When social interactions don't go as expected, it can trigger feelings of shame, frustration, or sadness.

3. Routine Disruptions: Change can be difficult for anyone, but for neurodivergent teens, it can be particularly unsettling. A disruption in routine can lead to feelings of confusion, anxiety, or even a sense of being out of control.

4. Cognitive Differences: Neurodivergent individuals often process information differently, which can sometimes make it hard to interpret emotions or social cues. This can lead to overthinking or misinterpreting situations, which in turn can heighten emotional responses.

The Connection Between Emotional Vulnerability and Emotional Dysregulation

Emotional dysregulation occurs when your emotional responses are more intense or last longer than what feels manageable. For neurodivergent teens, this can be a common experience. Imagine you're carrying a bucket of water (your emotions). When life is calm, the bucket is steady. But when stress, sensory overload, or unexpected changes occur, it's like someone is shaking the bucket, causing water to spill out—sometimes in the form of tears, anger, or withdrawal.

Understanding emotional vulnerability is the first step toward managing emotional dysregulation. By recognizing what shakes your bucket, you can begin to develop strategies to keep it steady, even when life feels overwhelming.

Picture yourself carrying a bucket of water. When things are calm, the water stays level. But as soon as you encounter stress—like a noisy environment or a difficult conversation—the water starts to slosh around. If enough stressors pile up, the water might spill over the edge, representing an emotional outburst. Learning to steady your bucket, or even finding ways to reduce the water level, is key to managing emotional vulnerability.

Strategies for Managing Emotional Vulnerability

1. Mindfulness: Practicing mindfulness helps you stay grounded in the present moment. It allows you to observe your emotions without immediately reacting to them. This can be especially helpful when you feel your emotional radar picking up too many signals.

2. Sensory Regulation: If sensory sensitivity contributes to your emotional vulnerability, finding ways to regulate your sensory input can be beneficial. This might include using sensory tools like fidget toys, weighted blankets, or noise-canceling headphones.

3. Routine and Structure: Creating a predictable routine can reduce feelings of anxiety and help you feel more in control. When you know what to expect, it can be easier to manage your emotions.

4. Social Support: Connecting with others who understand your experiences can be incredibly grounding. Whether it's a friend, family member, or therapist, having someone to talk to can help you process your emotions in a safe environment.

5. Self-Compassion: Remember that it's okay to feel deeply. Being emotionally vulnerable doesn't make you weak; it makes you human. Treat yourself with the same kindness and understanding you would offer a friend.

The Power of Self-Awareness

One of the most important tools in managing emotional vulnerability is self-awareness. The more you understand your emotional triggers and responses, the better equipped you'll be to handle them. This doesn't mean you'll never feel overwhelmed, but it does mean you'll have the tools to navigate those feelings in a healthier way.

Start by paying attention to your emotions throughout the day. Notice when you feel particularly vulnerable or when your emotions seem out of proportion to the situation. This awareness is the first step in taking control of your emotional responses.

Understanding and managing emotional vulnerability is a journey. It's about learning to embrace your sensitivity as a strength rather than seeing it as a weakness. By developing self-awareness and practicing the strategies outlined in this chapter, you'll be better equipped to handle the emotional waves that come your way.

Remember, it's okay to feel deeply. Your emotions are a part of who you are, and learning to navigate them is an important step toward living a balanced and fulfilling life. As you continue through this workbook, keep building on these skills, and know that each step you take is a step toward greater emotional resilience.

Exploring Your Emotional Triggers

Reflect on a recent experience where you felt emotionally overwhelmed or sensitive.
Answer the following questions to help you explore the situation in detail.

What happened?
Describe the event in one or two sentences.

What were you thinking?
Write down the thoughts that went through your mind during this time.

How did you feel?
List the emotions you experienced.

How did your body react?
Describe any physical sensations or changes in your body.

Chapter 4.3:

CHECK the Facts

Understanding and managing emotions can be tricky, especially when our feelings don't always match up with what's actually happening around us. In DBT, the "CHECK the Facts" skill helps you separate your emotions from the facts of a situation. This skill is crucial for managing intense feelings and reacting more effectively to challenging situations.

What is "CHECK the Facts"?

"CHECK the Facts" is a technique designed to help you assess whether your emotional response is based on facts or on your interpretations and assumptions. When we're overwhelmed, our feelings can cloud our judgment, making us believe things that may not be true. By checking the facts, you can identify whether your emotions are justified or if they might be a reaction to a misperception.

Why is "CHECK the Facts" Important?

1. Reduces Emotional Intensity: When emotions feel out of control, checking the facts can help ground you and reduce the intensity of your feelings.
2. Improves Decision Making: By focusing on what's actually happening, you can make more informed and effective decisions.

3. Enhances Self-Awareness: This skill helps you recognize when your emotions might be influenced by assumptions rather than reality.

3. Routine and Structure: Creating a predictable routine can reduce feelings of anxiety and help you feel more in control. When you know what to expect, it can be easier to manage your emotions.

4. Social Support: Connecting with others who understand your experiences can be incredibly grounding. Whether it's a friend, family member, or therapist, having someone to talk to can help you process your emotions in a safe environment.

5. Self-Compassion: Remember that it's okay to feel deeply. Being emotionally vulnerable doesn't make you weak; it makes you human. Treat yourself with the same kindness and understanding you would offer a friend.

The Power of Self-Awareness

One of the most important tools in managing emotional vulnerability is self-awareness. The more you understand your emotional triggers and responses, the better equipped you'll be to handle them. This doesn't mean you'll never feel overwhelmed, but it does mean you'll have the tools to navigate those feelings in a healthier way.

Start by paying attention to your emotions throughout the day. Notice when you feel particularly vulnerable or when your emotions seem out of proportion to the situation. This awareness is the first step in taking control of your emotional responses.

Understanding and managing emotional vulnerability is a journey. It's about learning to embrace your sensitivity as a strength rather than seeing it as a weakness. By developing self-awareness and practicing the strategies outlined in this chapter, you'll be better equipped to handle the emotional waves that come your way.

Remember, it's okay to feel deeply. Your emotions are a part of who you are, and learning to navigate them is an important step toward living a balanced and fulfilling life. As you continue through this workbook, keep building on these skills, and know that each step you take is a step toward greater emotional resilience.

Fact-Checking a Recent Emotional Response

Think of a recent situation where you felt strong emotions.
Fill in the details below:

Describe what happened that triggered your emotional response.

Identify the emotion you felt.

Write down any assumptions or interpretations you made.

List the objective facts related to the situation.

Compare your assumptions to the actual facts.

Based on the facts, describe how you can adjust your emotional response.

Chapter 4.4:

Opposite Action

Life is full of emotions, and sometimes those emotions can lead us to act in ways we don't really want to. "Opposite Action" is a skill from Dialectical Behavior Therapy (DBT) that helps you break the cycle of reacting automatically to your feelings by taking actions that go against your initial impulses. It's like hitting the reset button on your emotional responses, helping you find a healthier path forward.

What is "Opposite Action"?

"Opposite Action" involves doing something that is directly contrary to what your emotions are telling you to do. For instance, if you're feeling anxious and want to avoid a social event, the opposite action would be to go to the event and interact with others. The goal is to interrupt the cycle of unhelpful behavior and gradually change how you feel.

Why Use "Opposite Action"?

1. Breaks Unhelpful Patterns: Emotions can drive us to engage in negative or unproductive behaviors. By doing the opposite, you can disrupt these patterns.
2. Changes Emotional Responses: Acting against your emotional urges can shift your mood and reduce the intensity of the emotion.
3. Promotes Positive Actions: It encourages you to take actions that align with your goals and values, even when emotions try to pull you in a different direction.

How to Use "Opposite Action"

1. Identify the Emotion: Start by naming the emotion you're experiencing. Are you feeling angry, sad, or anxious?

2. Recognize the Urge: Notice what you feel like doing in response to this emotion. For example, if you're feeling depressed, you might want to withdraw from others.

3. Determine the Opposite Action: Think about the action that would be the opposite of what your emotions are pushing you toward. If your urge is to isolate, the opposite action could be reaching out to friends.

4. Act on the Opposite: Even if it feels uncomfortable, carry out the opposite action. Pay attention to how this action affects your feelings and the situation.

Imagine you're feeling overwhelmed with stress from school and want to avoid your homework. Using "Opposite Action," you might choose to set a timer for 15 minutes and start working on your homework. Instead of avoiding it, you engage with it, which can help reduce your stress and improve your sense of control.

Here's How It Works:

1. Emotion: Stress and overwhelm.
2. Natural Urge: To avoid homework.
3. Opposite Action: To work on the homework for a short, manageable period.
4. Action Taken: You set a timer for 15 minutes and start working. Afterward, you might find that the task feels more manageable and less overwhelming.

Opposite Action Reflection

Think of a past situation where your emotions influenced your actions negatively.
Complete the following sections in your workbook:

Describe what you did or wanted to do in response to the emotion.

Describe the situation and the emotion you felt.

Identify what the opposite action would have been.

Reflect on how taking the opposite action could have changed the situation.

Chapter 4.5:

Problem Solving

Problem-solving is like having a toolbox for dealing with life's challenges. It's a skill that helps you figure out practical ways to handle obstacles and make decisions that lead to better outcomes. This chapter will guide you through a structured way to solve problems effectively, making it easier to handle the tricky situations that come your way.

What is Problem Solving?

Problem-solving involves identifying a challenge, thinking through possible solutions, and choosing the best one to solve it. It's not just about finding a fix but also about approaching problems in a way that helps you feel more in control and less overwhelmed. Think of it as a step-by-step process to navigate obstacles and find your way to a solution.

Why Problem Solving Matters

1. Reduces Stress: Knowing how to solve problems can reduce the anxiety that comes from feeling stuck or overwhelmed.
2. Boosts Confidence: Successfully solving problems boosts your self-esteem and helps you feel more capable.
3. Improves Decision-Making: It helps you make informed choices by weighing the pros and cons of different options.
4. Promotes Independence: Effective problem-solving skills lead to greater independence by equipping you to handle challenges on your own.

The Problem-Solving Process

Here's a simple, step-by-step guide to solving problems effectively:

1. Define the Problem: Clearly understand what the problem is. Write down what's happening and why it's a problem.

Example: You're struggling with managing your time between schoolwork and hobbies. The problem is that you're always feeling rushed and missing out on activities you enjoy.

2. Brainstorm Possible Solutions: Think of all possible ways to address the problem. Don't judge or dismiss ideas at this stage; just list them out.

Example Solutions:
- Create a schedule that balances schoolwork and hobbies.
- Use a timer to manage study sessions and break times.
- Ask for help from a teacher or parent to prioritize tasks.

3. Evaluate and Choose a Solution: Look at each solution you've brainstormed. Consider the pros and cons, and think about how practical each option is.

Example:
- Creating a schedule might help you organize your time but may require adjusting your routine.
- Using a timer is easy to implement and helps manage time effectively.
- Asking for help could provide guidance but might not be necessary if you can manage the schedule on your own.

4. Implement the Solution: Put your chosen solution into action. Make a plan for how you'll carry it out.

Example: Decide to create a weekly schedule and set up a timer for study sessions.

5. Monitor and Reflect: After implementing the solution, check in to see how well it's working. Reflect on what's going well and what might need adjustment.

Example: After a week, review how well your schedule is helping you balance schoolwork and hobbies. Adjust the timing or tasks as needed.

6. Adjust if Necessary: If the solution isn't working as well as you hoped, revisit your brainstormed ideas and try another approach.

Example: If the timer isn't helping, consider using an app to track your time or find new ways to integrate hobbies into your schedule.

Personal Problem-Solving Plan

Identify a problem you're currently facing. It could be anything from managing your time to dealing with a conflict.

Describe the problem in detail.

List all potential solutions without judging them.

Consider the pros and cons of each solution and select the best one.

Describe how you will put the chosen solution into action.

Chapter 4.6:

Building Mastery and Coping Ahead

If you've made it this far in the workbook, give yourself a big high five. You're doing great! In this chapter, we're going to talk about two super cool skills that can help you feel more confident and prepared for whatever life throws your way. Let's dive into Building Mastery and Coping Ahead!

What's the Deal with Building Mastery?

Okay, so "Building Mastery" might sound like something out of a video game, right? Well, it's kind of like that, but for real life. It's all about getting better at stuff that matters to you. When you build mastery, you're basically leveling up your skills and confidence. And let me tell you, that feels pretty darn good!

Why Building Mastery Rocks for Neurodivergent Brains

If you're autistic or have ADHD, you might sometimes feel like the world isn't built for the way your brain works. Building mastery is a way to remind yourself that you're capable of awesome things. It can help you:

1. Boost your self-esteem
2. Reduce feelings of helplessness
3. Give you a sense of control
4. Provide a positive focus for your energy

Plus, many neurodivergent folks have special interests or hyperfixations. Building mastery is a great way to channel those interests into something that makes you feel good about yourself.

How to Build Mastery

Building mastery is all about setting goals and working towards them. Here's how you can get started:

1. Choose something you want to get better at: It could be anything from coding to cooking to playing a musical instrument.

2. Break it down into small steps: Don't try to become a master overnight. Small, consistent progress is the key.

3. Practice regularly: Even just 10-15 minutes a day can make a big difference over time.

4. Track your progress: Keeping a record can help you see how far you've come.

5. Celebrate your wins: Did you learn a new skill or reach a mini-goal? Do a happy dance!

Let's create a plan for building mastery in something you care about:

What skill do you want to improve?

Why is this important to you?

What's one small step you can take to start improving this skill?

How often will you practice? (Be realistic!)

How will you track your progress?

How will you celebrate your wins?

Remember, the goal isn't to be perfect. It's about making progress and feeling good about your efforts.

Alright, now let's talk about Coping Ahead. This skill is like having a secret playbook for life's tricky moments. It's all about preparing yourself for situations that might be challenging.

Why Coping Ahead is Awesome for Neurodivergent Brains

If you're neurodivergent, you might sometimes feel caught off guard by situations that others seem to handle easily. Coping Ahead can help you:

1. Feel more prepared and less anxious

2. Have strategies ready when you need them
3. Build confidence in your ability to handle challenges
4. Reduce the likelihood of meltdowns or shutdowns

How to Cope Ahead

Coping Ahead involves a few steps. Think of it like planning a mission (but way less stressful):

1. Identify the situation: What's coming up that might be challenging?

2. Visualize it in detail: Imagine the scenario as vividly as you can.

3. Notice your feelings: How does thinking about this situation make you feel?

4. Plan your coping strategies: What skills or tools can you use to handle it?

5. Imagine it going well: Picture yourself using your strategies successfully.

6. Practice: If possible, do a dry run or role-play the situation.

Chapter 4.7:

PLEASE Skills: Treating Physical Illness, Balanced Eating, Avoiding Mood-Altering Substances, Balanced Sleep, Exercise

Let's get started with PLEASE Skills section. If you're wondering why it's called "PLEASE," don't worry – it's not because we're begging you to do something (though we might gently encourage you). It's actually an acronym that stands for some super important ways to take care of yourself. Let's break it down:

- Physical illness (Treat it)
- Balanced Eating
- Avoid mood-altering substances
- Balanced Sleep
- Exercise

These skills might seem pretty basic, but trust me, they're like the secret sauce for feeling good and managing your emotions better. When your body feels good, your mind usually follows suit. So let's dive in and see how we can make these skills work for you!

Treating Physical Illness

Okay, let's start with the "P" in PLEASE – treating physical illness. Now, I know what you're thinking: "Duh, of course I'd treat an illness!" But here's the thing: sometimes when we're not feeling great mentally, we might ignore or downplay physical stuff that's bothering us.

Why It Matters

Your body and mind are connected like best buds. When one's not doing great, the other often feels it too. Think about the last time you had a cold – did you feel like your usual sparkly self? Probably not, right?

For us neurodivergent folks, physical discomfort can sometimes be extra tricky. Maybe sensory issues make it hard to pinpoint what's wrong, or executive function challenges make it tough to actually do something about it.

What You Can Do

1. Listen to your body: Set a daily "body check-in" alarm on your phone. Take a minute to scan from head to toe. Any aches? Pains? Weird feelings? Jot 'em down.

2. Keep track: Use a symptom tracker app or a section in your planner to note any ongoing issues. This can help you spot patterns and explain things to a doctor if needed.

3. Have a health buddy: Ask a parent, friend, or trusted adult to be your "health buddy." They can help you remember appointments or nudge you to take meds.

4. Create a self-care kit: Put together a box with things that help when you're not feeling great. Maybe some tea, a soft blanket, your favorite stim toy, and instructions for contacting your doctor.

Balanced Eating

Alright, onto the "L" and "E" – balanced eating. Now, I'm not here to lecture you about food pyramids or count your veggies. Eating, especially for neurodivergent peeps, can be complicated. Sensory issues, executive function challenges, and meds can all impact our relationship with food.

My Ideal Menu

Avoiding Mood-Altering Substances

Now for the "A" – avoiding mood-altering substances. This one's pretty straightforward, but super important. We're talking about staying away from stuff that can mess with your mind and emotions in unpredictable ways.

Why It Matters

Look, I get it. Sometimes the idea of altering your mood might seem tempting, especially if you're dealing with tough emotions or sensory overload. But here's the thing: substances like alcohol, drugs, or even too much caffeine can make it way harder to manage your emotions and use the DBT skills you're learning.

For neurodivergent brains, these substances can be extra tricky. They might interact weirdly with medications or amplify sensory issues. Plus, they can mess with your sleep, which we know is super important (more on that in a bit!).

What You Can Do

1. Know your risks: Learn about how different substances might affect your specific neurodivergence and any medications you take.

2. Plan for peer pressure: Come up with some go-to phrases for turning down substances if friends offer. Practice saying them out loud.

3. Find healthy alternatives: What are some safer ways to change your mood or deal with stress? Maybe it's listening to music, using a fidget toy, or going for a run.

4. Seek support: If you're struggling with substance use, don't be afraid to reach out for help. There are people and resources specifically for neurodivergent folks dealing with this.

Balanced Sleep

Alright, let's talk about the "S" – balanced sleep. I know, I know, sleep can be a real struggle for a lot of us neurodivergent folks. Racing thoughts, sensory issues, and time blindness can all make bedtime a challenge. But getting good sleep is like a superpower for your brain and emotions.

Why It Matters

Sleep isn't just about not being tired (though that's nice too). It's when your brain processes information, regulates emotions, and recharges for the next day. Not getting enough sleep can make you more irritable, anxious, and way more likely to have emotional meltdowns.

What You Can Do

1. Create a sleep sanctuary: Make your bedroom a calm, sensory-friendly zone. Think soft lighting, comfortable textures, and maybe some white noise if that helps you.

2. Develop a wind-down routine: Your brain needs time to switch gears. Try to do the same calming activities each night before bed to signal "sleep time" to your body.

3. Manage screen time: The blue light from phones and computers can mess with your sleep cycle. Try using blue light filters or switching to non-screen activities before bed.

4. Be consistent: Try to go to bed and wake up at similar times each day, even on weekends. Your body loves routines!

5. Talk to your doctor: If sleep is a persistent struggle, chat with your healthcare provider. There might be specific strategies or treatments that can help.

Design Your Ideal Bedtime Routine

Exercise

Last but definitely not least, we've got the final "E" – exercise. Now, before you groan and skip this section, hear me out! Exercise doesn't have to mean running marathons or lifting heavy weights. It's about finding ways to move your body that feel good to you.

Why It Matters

Moving your body isn't just about physical health. It's a powerful tool for managing emotions, reducing stress, and even improving focus. For neurodivergent brains, exercise can be especially helpful in regulating sensory input and boosting mood.

What You Can Do

1. Find your groove: The best exercise is the one you'll actually do. Maybe it's dancing in your room, going for walks, swimming, or doing yoga. Experiment to find what feels good.

2. Start small: Don't feel like you need to jump into an intense routine. Even 5-10 minutes of movement can make a difference.

3. Make it sensory-friendly: If certain environments are overwhelming, look for quieter spaces or times to exercise. Or create a comfy workout spot at home.

4. Use it as a tool: Learn to recognize when movement might help you. Feeling anxious? A quick walk might help. Need to focus? Try some jumping jacks before sitting down to work.

5. Celebrate effort, not just results: Every time you move your body, you're doing something good for your brain. Be proud of that!

CHAPTER 5
Interpersonal Effectiveness Skills

Chapter 5.1:

DEAR MAN: Describe, Express, Assert, Reinforce, Mindful, Appear Confident, Negotiate

DEAR MAN is actually a super helpful tool for communicating what you want or need, especially in tricky situations.

Let's break it down:

- Describe
- Express
- Assert
- Reinforce
- Mindful
- Appear confident
- Negotiate

Sounds like a lot, right? Don't sweat it. We're going to take it step by step, and by the end, you'll have a new superpower for navigating social situations. Trust me, this stuff is gold for us neurodivergent folks who sometimes struggle with communication.

Why DEAR MAN Matters

Before we jump in, let's talk about why this skill is so important. As neurodivergent teens, we sometimes have a hard time expressing ourselves clearly, especially when we're asking for something or setting boundaries. Maybe you've had moments where you tried to say what you wanted, but it came out all wrong, or you just couldn't find the words at all. DEAR MAN is like a script you can follow to make sure you get your point across effectively.

Breaking Down DEAR MAN

D - Describe

This is where you set the scene. You're telling the other person exactly what's going on, sticking to the facts without any judgment or emotion.

Example: Instead of saying, "You're always so loud and annoying," you might say, "When we're studying together, I notice that you often talk at full volume and play music without headphones."

Your turn: Think of a situation where you need to ask for something or set a boundary. How would you describe it objectively? Write it down below:

E - Express

Now it's time to share your feelings about the situation. This is where you get to say how the situation affects you emotionally.

Example: "When this happens, I feel overwhelmed and frustrated because it's hard for me to concentrate with all the noise."

Your turn: How does the situation you described make you feel? Express it here:

A - Assert

This is where you clearly state what you want to happen. Be specific and direct.

Example: "I would like us to agree on quiet study times where we both use headphones if we want to listen to music."

Your turn: What do you want to happen in your situation? Assert it here:

R - Reinforce

Explain the positive effects of your request being granted. How will it benefit the other person or your relationship?

Example: "If we can do this, I think we'll both be able to study more effectively, and I'll be much more relaxed hanging out with you."

Your turn: How would getting what you want benefit everyone involved? Write it down:

M - Mindful

Stay focused on your goal. It's easy to get sidetracked, especially if the other person gets defensive or brings up other issues. Keep steering the conversation back to your main point.

Example: If they start talking about how you sometimes leave dirty dishes in the sink, you might say, "I understand that's frustrating for you, and we can definitely talk about that later, but right now I'd like to focus on finding a solution for our study time."

Your turn: What might distract you from your goal in this conversation? How can you stay mindful and on track?

A - Appear Confident

This one can be tough, especially if you're feeling anxious. But remember, appearing confident doesn't mean you have to feel confident. It's about how you present yourself.

Some tips for appearing confident:
- Maintain eye contact (or look at the bridge of their nose if eye contact is uncomfortable)
- Speak clearly and at a steady pace
- Keep your body language open (uncrossed arms, shoulders back)
- Use a firm, but not aggressive, tone of voice

Your turn: What are some ways you can appear confident in your situation? List them here:

N - Negotiate

Be willing to give to get. If the other person can't meet your request fully, see if you can find a middle ground that works for both of you.

Example: "Okay, if using headphones all the time doesn't work for you, how about we agree on specific quiet hours during our study sessions?"

Your turn: What are some possible compromises in your situation? Brainstorm a few here:

Putting It All Together

Now that we've broken down each part of DEAR MAN, let's see how it all comes together. Here's an example of how you might use DEAR MAN to ask a teacher for extra time on an assignment:

D: "I noticed that the essay assignment is due next Friday, which is the same day as the big math test."

E: "I'm feeling really anxious about getting both of these done well in the time we have."

A: "I was wondering if it would be possible to have an extra two days to complete the essay?"

R: "This would allow me to focus on studying for the math test and then give the essay my full attention, which I think would result in better quality work for both."

M: (Staying focused on this request, even if the teacher brings up other assignments or past due dates)

A: (Speaking clearly, making eye contact, and using a respectful but firm tone)

N: "If an extra two days isn't possible, would one extra day be okay?"

See how that flows? It's clear, respectful, and gives the teacher all the information they need to make a decision.

Chapter 5.2:

GIVE: Gentle, Interested, Validate, Easy Manner

If you're thinking, "Uh, what's GIVE? I thought we were done with the acronyms," don't worry – I've got your back. GIVE is another super cool tool in your DBT toolkit, and it's all about how to keep your relationships strong and healthy.

So, what does GIVE stand for? Let's break it down:

- Gentle
- _Interested
- Validate
- Easy manner

Sounds pretty chill, right? That's because GIVE is all about creating a vibe that makes people want to be around you and talk to you. It's like a recipe for being a good friend, family member, or just an all-around awesome person to interact with.

Why GIVE Matters

Before we jump into the details, let's chat about why GIVE is so important, especially for us neurodivergent folks. Sometimes, social stuff can feel like trying to read a book in a language we don't know. We might come across as too blunt, or not show interest in the right way, or accidentally say something that hurts someone's feelings.

GIVE is like a cheat code for social interactions. It helps us navigate conversations and relationships in a way that makes other people feel good and want to keep hanging out with us. Plus, when we use GIVE, we often find that people are more willing to listen to us and help us out when we need it.

Breaking Down GIVE

G - Gentle

Being gentle is all about approaching people and situations with kindness and respect. It's like handling a delicate object – you want to be careful not to break it.

What Gentle Looks Like:
- Using a calm tone of voice
- Avoiding harsh words or insults
- Not making threats or demands
- Being patient, even when you're frustrated

What Gentle Doesn't Look Like:
- Yelling or raising your voice
- Using sarcasm or put-downs
- Making aggressive gestures
- Giving ultimatums

Your Turn: Think of a time when someone was gentle with you. How did it make you feel? Write it down here:

Now, think of a situation where you could be more gentle. How would you change your approach:

I - Interested

Being interested is about showing the other person that you care about what they're saying or doing. It's like being a detective, but instead of solving crimes, you're solving the mystery of what makes this person tick.

What Interested Looks Like:
- Asking questions about what the person is saying
- Making eye contact (if that's comfortable for you)
- Nodding or using other non-verbal cues to show you're listening
- Remembering details they've shared before and bringing them up

What Interested Doesn't Look Like:
- Constantly checking your phone while they're talking
- Interrupting to talk about yourself
- Looking bored or distracted
- Changing the subject abruptly

Your Turn: Think of someone you find really interesting:

What do you do to show them you're interested? List your behaviors here

Now, think of a conversation where you could have shown more interest. What would you do differently?

V - Validate

Validating is about letting the other person know that their feelings and experiences make sense. It's like saying, "I see you, I hear you, and what you're feeling is okay."

What Validating Looks Like:

- Acknowledging the other person's emotions
- Showing that you understand why they feel the way they do
- Not dismissing their experiences or feelings
- Expressing that their reaction is understandable

What Validating Doesn't Look Like:

- Telling someone they shouldn't feel a certain way
- Minimizing their experiences ("It's not a big deal")
- Trying to fix their problems right away without listening
- Comparing their struggles to others ("At least you don't have it as bad as...")

Your Turn: Think of a time when someone validated your feelings. What did they say or do? How did it make you feel?

Now, imagine a friend is upset about something you think is small. How could you validate their feelings?

E - Easy Manner

Having an easy manner is about being relaxed and approachable. It's like being a comfy couch that people want to sit on (metaphorically, of course – please don't let people sit on you).

What Easy Manner Looks Like:

- Using a relaxed tone of voice
- Smiling or using other friendly facial expressions
- Using humor when appropriate
- Being flexible and going with the flow

What Easy Manner Doesn't Look Like:

- Being rigid or inflexible
- Always being serious or intense
- Getting easily frustrated or upset
- Using an aggressive or confrontational tone

Your Turn: Think of someone you know who has an easy manner. What do they do that makes them easy to be around?

Now, think of a situation where you could have had an easier manner. How would you change your approach?

Chapter 5.3:

FAST: Fair, Apologies (no excessive), Stick to Values, Truthful

If you're thinking, "Another acronym? Seriously?" I feel you. But trust me, this one's pretty cool. FAST is all about keeping your self-respect while navigating relationships. It's like a superpower for standing up for yourself without burning bridges.

So, what does FAST stand for? Let's break it down:

- Fair
- Apologies (no excessive)
- Stick to values
- Truthful

Sounds pretty straightforward, right? But don't be fooled – there's a lot of power packed into these four little letters. FAST is your secret weapon for maintaining your integrity and self-respect, even when things get tricky.

Why FAST Matters

Before we dive into the nitty-gritty, let's chat about why FAST is such a big deal, especially for us neurodivergent folks. Sometimes, we might feel pressured to change who we are to fit in. Or we might struggle with knowing when to stand our ground and when to compromise. FAST gives us a clear roadmap for navigating these situations.

Using FAST helps us:
1. Keep our self-respect intact

Think of FAST as your personal bodyguard, protecting your values and self-worth. Cool, right?

Breaking Down FAST

F - Fair

Being fair is all about treating others (and yourself!) with respect and consideration. It's like being a good referee in the game of life – making sure everyone gets a fair shot.

What Fair Looks Like:
- Considering others' needs as well as your own
- Being willing to compromise when appropriate
- Avoiding "all or nothing" thinking
- Recognizing and respecting others' rights

What Fair Doesn't Look Like:
- Always putting others' needs before your own
- Expecting others to read your mind
- Holding grudges or seeking revenge
- Discriminating against others

Your Turn: Think of a situation where you were treated unfairly. How did it make you feel? Now, imagine how you could have made that situation fair for everyone involved.

A - Apologies (no excessive)

This one's about owning up to your mistakes without going overboard. It's like finding the sweet spot between "Sorry I exist" and "I'm never wrong."

What Appropriate Apologizing Looks Like:
- Acknowledging when you've made a mistake
- Expressing sincere regret for your actions
- Taking responsibility for the consequences
- Offering to make amends when appropriate

What Excessive Apologizing Looks Like:
- Apologizing for things that aren't your fault
- Saying sorry for having needs or feelings
- Using apologies to avoid conflict
- Apologizing repeatedly for the same thing

Your Turn: Think of a time when you apologized excessively. How did it make you feel? Now, rewrite that apology in a way that's sincere but not excessive.

S - Stick to values

Sticking to your values is about staying true to what's important to you, even when it's tough. It's like having an internal compass that always points to your true north.

What Sticking to Values Looks Like:
- Knowing what's important to you
- Making decisions based on your values
- Standing up for what you believe in
- Being willing to say no to things that go against your values

What Not Sticking to Values Looks Like:
- Changing your beliefs to please others
- Ignoring your gut feelings about right and wrong
- Going along with the crowd even when it feels wrong
- Compromising your integrity for short-term gains

Your Turn: List three of your core values. Now, think of a situation where you might be tempted to compromise one of these values. How could you stick to your value in that situation?

T - Truthful

Being truthful is about honesty – with others and with yourself. It's like being a human lie detector, but for your own words and actions.

What Being Truthful Looks Like:
- Saying what you mean and meaning what you say
- Admitting when you don't know something
- Being honest about your feelings and needs
- Avoiding lies, even "white lies" or lies by omission

What Not Being Truthful Looks Like:
- Telling lies to avoid conflict or discomfort
- Exaggerating or downplaying the truth
- Pretending to agree when you don't
- Hiding important information from others

Your Turn: Think of a time when you weren't completely truthful. What motivated you to be untruthful? How could you have handled the situation honestly?

Chapter 5.5:

Self-Advocacy Techniques

So, what exactly is self-advocacy? Simply put, it's about speaking up for yourself and your needs. It's like being your own personal superhero, cape and all (okay, the cape is optional, but totally cool if you want one).

As a neurodivergent person, you might sometimes feel like the world isn't quite built for your brain. That's where self-advocacy comes in. It's about making sure your voice is heard and your needs are met.

Quick Activity: Your Self-Advocacy Superpowers

Before we dive deeper, let's warm up those self-advocacy muscles. Grab your pen and jot down:

1. Three things you're really good at
2. Three things you find challenging
3. One accommodation or support that really helps you

Great job! Knowing your strengths, challenges, and what helps you is the first step in self-advocacy. You just flexed those self-awareness muscles!

The ABCs of Self-Advocacy

Let's break down self-advocacy into three easy-to-remember steps: Awareness, Bravery, and Communication. We'll call it the ABCs of self-advocacy.

A is for Awareness

First things first, you gotta know yourself. What makes you tick? What sends you into sensory overload? What helps you focus? Being aware of your needs is like having a roadmap for your brain.

Activity: Create Your Neurodivergent Profile

Time to make a cool profile of your neurodivergent awesomeness.

1. My Strengths (e.g., amazing memory for facts about dinosaurs)
2. My Challenges (e.g., gets overwhelmed in noisy places)
3. Things That Help Me (e.g., noise-canceling headphones)
4. My Accommodation Needs (e.g., need extra time for tests)

Fill it out and decorate it however you want. This is your personal neurodivergent profile - it's as unique as you are!

My Strength	My Challenges	Things that Help me	My Accommodation Needs

B is for Bravery

Okay, let's be real. Speaking up for yourself can be scary sometimes. It takes guts to tell someone what you need, especially if you're worried they might not understand. But remember, you have the right to be heard and to have your needs met.

Bravery Boosters

Here are some tricks to help you feel braver:

1. Practice power poses: Stand like Superman or Wonder Woman for two minutes. It might feel silly, but research shows it can actually boost your confidence!

2. Use positive self-talk: Instead of "I can't do this," try "I've got this!" or "I'm nervous, but I can handle it."

3. Visualize success: Imagine the conversation going well. Picture the person listening and understanding.

4. Remember your why: Think about why self-advocacy is important to you. Maybe it's to do better in school, or to feel more comfortable in social situations.

C is for Communication

Alright, you're aware of your needs and you've got your bravery on. Now it's time to communicate! This is where all those interpersonal skills we've been practicing come in handy.

The POWER Method of Self-Advocacy Communication

Let's use a simple method called POWER to help structure your self-advocacy communication:

P	**Prepare: Know what you want to say before you say it.**
O	**Open with confidence: Start strong with a clear, confident statement.**
W	**W - Watch your tone: Stay calm and respectful, even if you're feeling frustrated.**
E	**E - Explain clearly: Use specific examples to illustrate your needs.**
R	**R - Request action: Clearly state what you need or what you'd like to happen.**

Let's see how this might look in action:

Scenario: You're struggling to keep up with note-taking in class because the teacher speaks too fast.

Using POWER:
Prepare: Write down key points you want to make.
Open: "Mr. Johnson, I'd like to talk to you about the pace of lectures in class."
Watch your tone: Speak calmly and respectfully.
Explain: "I'm having trouble keeping up with note-taking because the pace is quite fast for me. This means I'm missing important information."
Request: "Would it be possible to get copies of the lecture notes, or to slow down the pace a bit?"

Activity: POWER Practice

Think of a situation where you need to self-advocate. Use the POWER method to write out what you might say. Remember, practice makes progress!

Self-Advocacy in Different Settings

Now that we've got the basics down, let's look at how to use these skills in different parts of your life.

At School

School can be tough sometimes, especially when you're neurodivergent. But with self-advocacy, you can make it work better for you.

Tips for self-advocating at school:
1. Know your rights: Learn about the accommodations you're entitled to.
2. Build a support team: Identify teachers, counselors, or staff members who can help you.
3. Be specific about your needs: Instead of "I need help," try "I need extra time on tests" or "I need a quiet place to work sometimes."
4. Use "I" statements: "I learn best when..." or "I struggle with..."

Activity: Create Your School Self-Advocacy Plan

In your workbook, create a "School Self-Advocacy Plan." Include:
1. Three accommodations that would help you most
2. The names of two supportive staff members
3. A script for requesting one of your accommodations

With Friends and Peers

Friendships are awesome, but they can also be tricky to navigate sometimes. Self-advocacy can help you have better, more understanding relationships.

Tips for self-advocating with friends:
1. Be open about your neurodivergence (if you're comfortable)

2. Explain your needs clearly: "Loud places overwhelm me, can we hang out somewhere quieter?"
3. Suggest alternatives that work for you: "Instead of going to the mall, want to watch a movie at my place?"
4. Set boundaries: It's okay to say no to things that don't work for you

Activity: Friend Communication Cards

Create some "Friend Communication Cards" in your workbook. On each card, write:
1. A challenge you sometimes face in social situations
2. How it affects you
3. What your friends can do to help

These can be super helpful for explaining your needs to friends!

At Home

Home should be your safe space, but sometimes family members might not fully understand your needs. Self-advocacy can help create a more supportive home environment.

Tips for self-advocating at home:
1. Educate your family about neurodivergence
2. Explain how certain things affect you: "When there's a lot of background noise, it's hard for me to focus on homework."
3. Suggest solutions: "Could I have a quiet study space in my room?"
4. Appreciate their efforts: Thank your family when they accommodate your needs

Activity: Family Meeting Prep

Prepare for a family meeting to discuss your needs. In your workbook, write down:
1. Three things you'd like your family to understand about your neurodivergence
2. Two challenges you face at home
3. Two solutions or accommodations you'd like to suggest

Dealing with Pushback

Sometimes, even when you advocate for yourself perfectly, you might face some pushback. People might not understand or might be resistant to change. That's okay - it doesn't mean you've failed or that you should give up.

Strategies for Handling Pushback

1. Stay calm: Take a deep breath. Remember, this isn't a reflection on you.
2. Restate your needs: Sometimes people need to hear things more than once.
3. Ask questions: Try to understand their perspective. "Can you help me understand your concerns?"
4. Offer compromise: See if there's a middle ground that can work for everyone.
5. Seek support: If you're struggling, reach out to a trusted adult or advocate.

Activity: Pushback Scenarios

Let's practice handling pushback. In your workbook, write responses to these scenarios:

Your teacher says,

Dealing with Pushback

A friend says,

Here is another scenario:

Your parents say,

Advocating for yourself is important, but what's more important is how you do it. Use the communication techniques learnt in this workbook to advocate for yourself effectively.

CHAPTER 6
Integrating DBT Skills for Neurodivergent Living

Chapter 6.1

Creating a Personalized DBT-Informed Toolkit

This is the part where we get to build something totally unique - your very own DBT toolkit. Think of it like customizing your favorite video game character or putting together the perfect playlist. Only this time, we're crafting a set of tools that'll help you navigate life's twists and turns.

So, what exactly is a DBT-informed toolkit? Well, it's kinda like your personal Swiss Army knife for emotions and situations. Instead of blades and screwdrivers, though, you'll be packing skills and strategies that work best for your neurodivergent brain. Cool, right?

Let's dive in and start building your toolkit, piece by piece!

Step 1: Taking Stock of What You've Got

Before we start throwing new stuff in your toolkit, let's check out what you've already got. Grab a notebook or open up a fresh doc on your device. We're gonna make a list:

1. Skills you've learned so far
2. Strategies that have worked for you in the past
3. Things that help you feel calm or centered
4. People or resources you can turn to when things get tough

Step 2: Identifying Your Unique Needs

Okay, so here's the deal - your brain is as unique as your fingerprint. What works for your bestie might not work for you, and that's totally cool. The trick is figuring out what your specific needs are

Think about the situations that tend to trip you up. Maybe it's:
- Sensory overload in noisy places
- Difficulty switching between tasks
- Intense emotions that seem to come out of nowhere
- Challenges with social interactions

Step 3: Matching Skills to Your Needs

Time to play matchmaker! We're gonna pair up those tricky situations with DBT skills that might help. Don't worry if you don't remember all the skills - we'll do a quick recap.

Mindfulness Skills:
- Observe: Notice without reacting
- Describe: Put words to your experience
- Participate: Fully engage in the moment

Distress Tolerance Skills:
- TIPP: Temperature, Intense exercise, Paced breathing, Paired muscle relaxation
- ACCEPTS: Activities, Contributing, Comparisons, Emotions, Pushing away, Thoughts, Sensations
- Self-soothe with your senses

Emotion Regulation Skills:
- Check the Facts
- Opposite Action
- Problem Solving
- PLEASE: PhysicaL illness treatment, balanced Eating, avoid mood-Altering substances, balanced Sleep, Exercise

Interpersonal Effectiveness Skills:
- DEAR MAN: Describe, Express, Assert, Reinforce, Mindful, Appear confident, Negotiate
- GIVE: Gentle, Interested, Validate, Easy manner
- FAST: Fair, no Apologies, Stick to values, Truthful

Skill Matchmaking

Look at your list of challenging situations. For each one, try to match it with at least one skill that might help. Don't stress if you're not sure - we're just brainstorming here!

Example:
Challenge: Sensory overload at the mall
Possible skills:
- Mindfulness: Observe without judgment
- Distress Tolerance: Self-soothe with senses (noise-canceling headphones)
- Emotion Regulation: PLEASE (taking breaks to regulate)

Your turn! Match your challenges with potential skills:

CHALLENGE	POSSIBLE SKILL

Chapter 6.2:

Applying DBT Skills to Daily Neurodivergent Challenges

Let's take all those cool DBT skills you've been learning and put them to work in your everyday life. It's like taking your superpowers out for a test drive!

Living with a neurodivergent brain can sometimes feel like playing a video game on hard mode. But guess what? You've been leveling up your skills, and now it's time to use them to tackle those daily challenges. Let's dive in and see how we can make your life a little easier and a whole lot more awesome!

Understanding Your Daily Challenges

First things first, let's talk about what kinds of challenges you might face on the regular. Every neurodivergent person is unique, but there are some common hurdles that many of us deal with. Maybe you can relate to some of these:

1. Sensory overload in noisy or crowded places
2. Difficulty with transitions or unexpected changes
3. Trouble focusing on tasks or getting started
4. Managing intense emotions
5. Navigating social situations
6. Dealing with executive function struggles (like organizing or time management)
7. Coping with anxiety or depression

Take a moment to jot down 5 challenges that you often face in your day-to-day life. Be specific!

Awesome job! Now we know exactly what we're working with.

Managing Transitions and Unexpected Changes

For many neurodivergent folks, changes in routine can feel like someone just flipped the game board. But we've got some strategies to help you roll with the punches!

The "Radical Acceptance" skill from distress tolerance can be a game-changer here. It doesn't mean you have to like the change, just that you're acknowledging it's happening. Try saying to yourself, "This is happening, even though I don't like it."

You can also use the "Check the Facts" skill from emotion regulation:
1. What's the situation?
2. What are my interpretations or assumptions?
3. What are the actual facts?
4. What's the worst that could happen? The best? The most likely?

Think of a recent unexpected change or transition that was tough for you. Let's break it down:

Describe the change

Your initial reaction

Use "Check the Facts" - what were the actual facts of the situation?

Practice Radical Acceptance - write an acceptance statement:

Chapter 6.3:

Progress Tracking and Self-Reflection

You've been putting in some serious work, and now it's time to talk about how we can keep track of all that progress you're making.

Think of this chapter as your personal game stats tracker. You know how in video games you can see how many coins you've collected or levels you've beaten? Well, we're going to set up something similar for your DBT skills. It's gonna be cool, I promise!

Why Track Your Progress?

Now, you might be thinking, "Ugh, more work?" But hear me out. Tracking your progress is like having a highlight reel of your own awesomeness. Here's why it's super helpful:

1. It shows you how far you've come (even when it doesn't feel like it)
2. It helps you spot patterns in what works for you
3. It gives you a boost of motivation when you're feeling stuck
4. It helps you set goals and crush them

Plus, it's a great way to practice that mindfulness we've been talking about. You'll be paying attention to your experiences in a whole new way!

Setting Up Your Progress Tracker

Alright, let's get down to business. We're going to create a progress tracker that works for your unique brain. Some people love writing things down, others prefer digital tools, and some might want to draw or use stickers. Whatever floats your boat!

Skill Usage Tracker

This is where you'll keep tabs on which DBT skills you're using in your daily life. It's like leveling up your character in a role-playing game!

Your Skill Usage Tracker

Skill	Mon	Tue	Wed	Thur	Fri	Sat	Sun
Mindfulness							
Distress Tolerance							
Emotion Regulation							
Interpersonal Effectiveness							

CHAPTER 7
Resources

Chapter 7.1

Additional DBT and Neurodivergence Support

This chapter is all about hooking you up with extra support and cool stuff to keep your DBT skills growing. Think of it as your personal toolkit for navigating the wild world of being a neurodivergent teen.

Online Communities and Forums

Sometimes, you just need to connect with people who get it. Here are some online hangouts where you can chat with other neurodivergent teens and DBT enthusiasts:

1. Reddit Communities
   - r/dbtselfhelp: A supportive space for sharing DBT experiences and tips.
   - r/neurodiversity: Celebrate all kinds of minds here!
   - r/autism and r/ADHD: Specific communities for autistic and ADHD folks.

2. Discord Servers
   - "Neurodivergent and Proud": A teen-friendly server for neurodivergent peeps.
   - "DBT Skills Group": Practice your skills with others in real-time.

3. Facebook Groups
   - "DBT for Neurodivergent Teens": A private group for sharing and support.
   - "Autistic and ADHD Teens Unite": Connect with other teens like you.

These online spaces can be great for sharing experiences, asking questions, and finding support from people who understand what you're going through. Just remember to stay safe online and respect the rules of each community.

Apps and Digital Tools

Your phone can be a DBT powerhouse! Check out these apps to keep your skills sharp:

1. DBT Diary Card and Skills Coach: Track your moods and practice skills on the go.
2. Calm Harm: Great for managing urges and distress tolerance.
3. Mindfulness for Teens: Guided meditations tailored for the teenage brain.
4. Habitica: Turn your DBT practice into a fun RPG-style game.
5. Forest: Stay focused during mindfulness exercises by growing virtual trees.

These apps can help you practice your DBT skills anywhere, anytime. They're like having a mini-therapist in your pocket!

Podcasts and YouTube Channels

For those times when reading just isn't your jam, tune into these audio and video resources:

Podcasts:
1. "Neurodiversity Podcast": Celebrating different ways of thinking.
2. "The Autism Show": Real talk about life on the spectrum.
3. "ADHD reWired": Strategies and stories for the ADHD brain.
4. "The Mindset Mentor": Quick doses of motivation and mindfulness.

YouTube Channels:
1. "How to ADHD": Fun and informative videos about living with ADHD.
2. "Yo Samdy Sam": Autistic perspectives and life hacks.

3. "DBT Peer Connections": Real people sharing DBT experiences.
4. "Therapy in a Nutshell": Mental health tips in bite-sized videos.

These audio and video resources can be great for learning on the go or when you need a break from reading.

Local Support Groups and Workshops

Sometimes, it's awesome to connect with people face-to-face. Here are some ideas for finding in-person support:

1. Check with your school counselor about teen support groups.
2. Look for DBT skills groups at local mental health clinics.
3. See if there's an Autism or ADHD support group in your area.
4. Ask your therapist about group therapy options.
5. Look for mindfulness or meditation workshops at community centers.

In-person groups can provide a sense of community and give you a chance to practice your social skills in a supportive environment.

Advocacy Organizations

Want to make a difference? These organizations are working to support neurodivergent folks:

1. Autistic Self Advocacy Network (ASAN): Run by and for autistic people.
2. CHADD: Support and resources for people with ADHD.
3. National Alliance on Mental Illness (NAMI): Offers support groups and education.
4. The Trevor Project: Support for LGBTQ+ youth, including those who are neurodivergent.

Getting involved with advocacy can help you feel empowered and connected to the larger neurodivergent community.

Crisis Resources

Sometimes things get really tough, and that's okay. Here are some places you can turn to for immediate support:

1. Crisis Text Line: Text HOME to 741741 for 24/7 support.
2. National Suicide Prevention Lifeline: Call 1-800-273-8255 anytime.
3. The Trevor Project Lifeline: Call 1-866-488-7386 for LGBTQ+ youth support.
4. Your local emergency services: Don't hesitate to call 911 if you're in danger.

It's important to have these resources on hand, just in case. Remember, reaching out for help is a sign of strength, not weakness.

Neurodiversity-Affirming Therapists

Finding a therapist who really gets neurodivergence can be a game-changer. Here are some tips for finding the right fit:

1. Look for therapists who specifically mention working with autism or ADHD.
2. Ask potential therapists about their experience with DBT and neurodivergence.
3. Check out directories like Psychology Today or the International OCD Foundation for therapist listings.
4. Don't be afraid to "shop around" - it's okay to try a few sessions with different therapists to find the right match.

A good therapist can be a valuable ally in your journey, so it's worth taking the time to find someone who understands your unique needs.

Appendix

Glossary of DBT Terms

A

Acceptance: Recognizing reality for what it is without trying to change it. It's like looking at a rainy day and saying, "Yep, it's raining," instead of wishing it was sunny.

Accumulate Positive Experiences: Building up good stuff in your life to make you more resistant to negative emotions. It's like filling up your "happiness bank account."

ACCEPTS: A distress tolerance skill. It stands for Activities, Contributing, Comparisons, Emotions, Pushing Away, Thoughts, and Sensations. It's your toolkit for getting through tough moments.

Alternate Rebellion: Finding safe ways to rebel that don't hurt you or others. It's like dyeing your hair purple instead of skipping school.

Analyze: Breaking down a problem or situation to understand it better. It's like being a detective in your own life.

B

Behavior Chain Analysis: A step-by-step breakdown of what led to a specific behavior. It's like creating a map of your actions and thoughts.

Biosocial Theory: The idea that some people are born more emotionally sensitive and that their environment can make this sensitivity better or worse. It's like having a mood thermostat that's extra responsive.

Building Mastery: Doing things that make you feel competent and effective. It's like leveling up in a video game, but for real life skills.

C

Check the Facts: An emotion regulation skill where you make sure your emotional response matches the situation. It's like being a fact-checker for your feelings.

Cognitive Restructuring: Changing negative thought patterns to more balanced ones. It's like giving your brain a makeover.

Core Mindfulness: The foundation of all DBT skills, focusing on being aware and present in the moment. It's like being the director of your own life movie.

Crisis Survival Skills: Techniques to help you get through intense, difficult situations without making them worse. It's your emotional emergency kit.

D

DBT: Stands for Dialectical Behavior Therapy. It's a type of therapy that helps people manage intense emotions and improve relationships.

DEAR MAN: An interpersonal effectiveness skill for asking for what you want. It stands for Describe, Express, Assert, Reinforce, Mindful, Appear confident, and Negotiate.

Dialectics: The idea that two seemingly opposite things can both be true. It's like recognizing that you can be both strong and vulnerable at the same time.

Distress Tolerance: Skills for coping with painful events and emotions when you can't make things better right away. It's like having a sturdy umbrella in an emotional storm.

E

Emotion Mind: When your thoughts and actions are controlled mainly by your emotions. It's like your feelings are in the driver's seat.

Emotion Regulation: Skills for changing or managing your emotions. It's like being the DJ of your own mood music.

Evaluate: Assessing the pros and cons of a situation or potential action. It's like being a judge in the courtroom of your choices.

F

FAST: An interpersonal effectiveness skill for maintaining self-respect. It stands for Fair, Apologies (no excessive), Stick to values, and Truthful.

Feelings Thermometer: A tool to measure the intensity of your emotions. It's like having a mood weather report.

G

GIVE: An interpersonal effectiveness skill for building and maintaining positive relationships. It stands for Gentle, Interested, Validate, and Easy manner.

Grounding Techniques: Methods to connect with the present moment and reduce anxiety. It's like dropping an anchor when your mind is stormy.

H

Half-Smile: A technique where you relax your face into a slight smile to help change your mood. It's like tricking your brain into feeling a bit better.

I

Interpersonal Effectiveness: Skills for maintaining relationships and self-respect while achieving your objectives. It's like being a diplomat in your personal life.

Invalidating Environment: A setting that dismisses or rejects a person's emotional experiences. It's like living in a world that keeps saying "You shouldn't feel that way."

L

Linehan, Marsha: The creator of DBT. She's like the Steve Jobs of emotional regulation techniques.

M

Mindfulness: Paying attention to the present moment without judgment. It's like being a friendly observer of your own life.

N

Non-Judgmental Stance: Observing without labeling things as good or bad. It's like being a neutral sports commentator for your life events.

O

Observe: A mindfulness skill where you notice your experiences without trying to change them. It's like being a wildlife photographer of your own thoughts and feelings.

Opposite Action: Doing the opposite of what your emotion is telling you to do. It's like steering your emotional car in the reverse direction.

P

PLEASE Skills: Emotion regulation techniques focused on taking care of your physical health. It stands for treat PhysicaL illness, balanced

Sleep, and Exercise.

Primary Emotions: The first, immediate emotional reaction to a situation. It's like the first domino to fall in a line of emotional reactions.

R

Radical Acceptance: Completely accepting reality as it is, without fighting against it. It's like embracing a rainstorm instead of complaining that it's not sunny.

Reasonable Mind: Thinking logically and rationally. It's like being Mr. Spock from Star Trek.

Regular Emotions: Day-to-day emotions that don't overwhelm you. It's like the background music of your emotional life.

S

Secondary Emotions: Emotional reactions to your primary emotions. It's like feeling angry about feeling sad.

Self-Soothe: Using your five senses to calm yourself down. It's like giving yourself a mini-spa treatment for your emotions.

Skillful Means: Using the most effective method to achieve your goals. It's like choosing the right tool for an emotional job.

STOP Skill: A crisis survival strategy. It stands for Stop, Take a step back, Observe, and Proceed mindfully. It's like having an emotional pause button.

T

Target Behaviors: Specific actions or habits you're working to change. It's like having a "most wanted" list for behaviors you want to improve.

TIPP Skills: Crisis survival techniques that change your body chemistry. It stands for Temperature, Intense exercise, Paced breathing, and Paired muscle relaxation. It's like hitting the reset button on your nervous system.

V

Validation: Recognizing and accepting someone's feelings or experiences as understandable. It's like giving a thumbs up to someone's emotions, even if you don't agree with them.

Values: Principles that guide your decisions and behaviors. They're like your personal North Star.

W

Willfulness: Refusing to accept reality or trying to fix every problem immediately. It's like trying to paddle upstream against a strong current.

Willingness: Being open to experiencing reality as it is and doing what's effective. It's like going with the flow of a river.

Wise Mind: The balance between emotion mind and reasonable mind. It's like being the wise owl of your own life.

Blank DBT Worksheets for Continued Practice

Write your thoughts or just sketch freely here:

Great job, champ!

You've made it to the very end of this journey.

We're excited to offer you the audio version of this book for free as a reward for your commitment to self-discovery and self-development.

It is my dream that this audiobook become instrumental in your understanding and application of the concepts in this book.

Rooting for you!

Scan The QR Code To Get AudioBook

ABOUT THE PUBLISHER

Soul Sergeants is a dedicated team of mental health professionals and educators focused on promoting emotional wellness and psychological resilience. Our mission is to provide accessible, engaging, and effective resources for individuals of all ages—children, teenagers, and adults. We offer a range of products including workbooks, tools, and digital resources, all designed to address various mental health and emotional challenges. Our approach is grounded in evidence-based therapeutic strategies such as Dialectical Behavior Therapy (DBT), Cognitive Behavioral Therapy (CBT), and Acceptance and Commitment Therapy (ACT) and others.

Our multidisciplinary team comprises licensed therapists, counselors, psychologists, psychiatrists, and designers, ensuring that our resources are psychologically sound, visually appealing, and age-appropriate. At Soul Sergeants, we believe that mental and emotional wellness is a journey, not a destination. Our philosophy centers on empowering individuals with knowledge and skills, encouraging self-discovery, fostering resilience, and promoting a positive, proactive approach to mental health. By choosing Soul Sergeants, customers join a community dedicated to mental and emotional wellness, working together towards a future where emotional well-being is accessible to all.

Soul Sergeants

We'd Love Your Feedback:

We've invested considerable effort and expertise in crafting this workbook to provide you with the best possible resource. As an added benefit, we've created an audio version that you can access for free, allowing you to engage with the material in a way that suits your learning style.

Please let us know if this workbook made a positive impact on your life. Has this resource helped or improved you in some way? If so, we'd be grateful to hear about your experience. Your honest feedback not only helps us improve but also assists other readers in finding the right resources for their needs. By sharing your thoughts, you're helping fellow readers make informed decisions.

To leave a review, simply go to our product page on Amazon by searching 'Soul Sergeants" on Amazon. Locate this title and leave your thoughts in the review section. Your insights are invaluable, and we appreciate you taking the time to share them.

Made in United States
Troutdale, OR
05/05/2025

31096798R00104